GW00730478

Putting It Out There

Life in Full Swing

Putting It Out There

Life in Full Swing

Andy Griffiths

About the Author

Andy Griffiths is a UK-born PGA golf professional, amateur photo bomber, and full-time life lover. When lack of height stopped his dream of playing professional football in its tracks, the local golf course became his second home. He realised he had a talent for the sport and, after many hours of practice, competition and improvement, he turned professional and studied for a degree in Applied Golf Management at the University of Birmingham. After his initial attempts at undergraduate essays there, it's quite ironic that he's now a published author! Inspired by the many opportunities in the huge world of golf, Andy has been able to spend time as a teaching professional in many fantastic places through utilising the power of social media, networking, and a growing reputation. Mixing his love of golf and travel, Andy has coached all over the world, including aboard a cruise ship during a 100 day world tour, and at many of the world's finest golf courses and academies across Europe, Asia, and America. He has shadowed and learned from many of the best coaches around the world in order to further improve his coaching. However, even for such a committed golfer, there is much more to life!

When not golfing, Andy can be found behind a drum kit, or reading, cooking, eating, learning new skills, practicing Mandarin, exercising, training for the upcoming North Korean marathon, getting lost and discovering new places in his own city, or on a plane heading somewhere new to explore. He is getting ever closer to visiting every country and aims to live this life as well as is humanly possible.

A Few Thanks

There are far too many people to thank you all personally. I've been blessed beyond measure to have such an abundance of family, friends and acquaintances whose positive influences have helped shape me.

Special thanks must go to Mum, Dad and big bro Jon, for supporting me through whatever crazy decisions I've made and always being there for a Skype chat and advice. I am realising now, more and more, that you have taught me so many lessons through your actions and example.

To the many people I have met through school, college, university, placements, social media, church, the cruise ship, living abroad, travelling, holidays, golf, competitions, coaching and more; you probably have no idea how each of you have impacted me in so many different ways.

To the contacts and now great friends I have made in the golf industry, who have helped me to develop far quicker than I could ever have imagined; your willingness to give freely and help my growth will stick with me forever, as I now also attempt to 'pay it forward'.

To the teachers, coaches, mentors and influences who made me realise that helping others, through coaching, was a useful career to follow: I think you were right.

To all those who have not forgotten little old me as I jetted off to the Middle Kingdom, and who didn't abandon, block or ignore me, despite my excess of pictures and posts; you have made me feel extremely loved with messages, calls, visits, gift boxes and more, and helped make settling into China more manageable than I ever imagined.

To the fellow expats, my boss, company and co-workers, my new friends, and everyone who is and has been alongside me here in China, and been a part of this adventure.

To the Chinese people I come across each day, you never stop surprising me with your unique mix of generosity, hospitality, humour and randomness, which helped me to create countless stories as you welcomed a lǎowài/foreigner into your country.

Some of the people I've been fortunate to spend time with and have helped me in my life so far.

Finally, to those who supported and encouraged me to get my experiences and thoughts down on paper and contributed to my aim of helping as many people as I possibly could by writing this book, I am eternally grateful. To Mark, David and Woody for your help in prepping and editing pics. To Sarah, editor extraordinaire, your eight edits, endless chats, brainstorms and coming up with the end title (after huge inspiration from Sean) transformed this from feeling like an enthusiastic 6½ year old had written it. To Jane, graphic designer aka magic worker, your cover design, interior visuals and organising my madness brought it all together to look like a real book in a way far beyond what I ever imagined.

Thank you.

If I missed you… I still love you and believe me, I am grateful.

Edited by Sarah Graham (sarah-graham.co.uk)
Designed by Jane Warring (linkedin.com/in/janewarringgraphicdesign)

Introduction

Life is an adventure. It's a cliché that's as true as you make it, but for me it's been a guiding principle. My love of travel, challenges and new experiences, combined with my passion for helping people, has led me to some fantastic places, stretched me beyond the limits of my comfort zone, and taught so much about life and the world beyond my English upbringing.

I'm a golf professional who coaches full-time, but this book is not about golf. It won't teach you new and improved techniques for your swing, or how to perfect your putting, but it will share some of the many life lessons I've learnt during my adventure so far, which I feel can help your life – and your golf too, if you want to apply it in that way. I was born and raised in England but, over the course of my career, have been fortunate enough to travel and work all around the world, and to meet some truly incredible people who have shaped me into an inquisitive life-lover, determined to leave the world a little bit better than when I arrived here.

My adventure took an altogether new direction when I moved 6,000 miles to start a new chapter of my life in China. No matter how much travelling you've done, and how travel-smart you believe you are, nothing can fully prepare you for the shock of moving somewhere so vastly different from everything you're used to. This book is, in part, a way of chronicling this leg of my adventure and, I hope, gives an insight into the baffling, amusing, occasionally frustrating, and often surreal experience of life in China.

My job involves constantly striving to better myself so that I can offer my players the absolute best. As a coach, there's not much that fires me up more than the opportunity to improve the lives of others in any small way. Whether it's by passing on an infectious smile; helping people grow in confidence as they realise what they can achieve; or giving advice on what can and can't be controlled, and the effects this can have on your happiness, my role as a coach is often far greater than simply improving my players' golf technique or golf-related earnings. Knowing that I can help to positively shape the lives of those around me is what I'm addicted to – that, and living life to the fullest, filling it with all kinds of fun and excitement.

I hope this book can also offer some comfort and perspective to those facing some of life's biggest, most challenging changes – be that a change of home, career, relationship, or any other of life's big 'crossroad' decisions. Life in China has certainly been a huge adjustment, but also a fantastic opportunity for me to progress. So there you have it: this book is a way to showcase the madness, exhilaration, challenges and triumphs of living in China, alongside some reflections than can hopefully help you too.

I've written the book as a number of individual stories, followed by a reflection on how they can apply to you and your life, and finally a call to action – something you can do to make that change. With the 52 stories, (and one bonus) I would recommend picking one story a week, reading through it, and then getting to the action point. Let it become a habit and give yourself time to really delve into each action point, as well as time for personal reflection on how it can best be applied to you and your individual situation. I hope you get lots out of this book. It was a lot of fun to write, and even more fun to experience it all. Live life to the fullest, and make sure you visit Shanghai sometime to create your own China stories. Enjoy the ride!

The Bund, Shanghai – the famous waterfront regarded as the symbol of Shanghai for hundreds of years

Lesson #1

Change may be scary, but no change is scarier

Today is the day. Almost 60kg of my life has been packed and, as I sit in the plane, it has finally hit me that the next time I set foot on land it will be in Asia – my base for at least the next two years. I have been lucky enough to travel to more than 60 countries in my life so far; however, despite having weighed up this move, and seen that it works out as a huge opportunity in so many ways, of course there is a little part of me that feels reluctant to go. And yeah… a little scared.

If I were to stay 'safe' within my comfort zone, turn back off the plane and live out my life in England, it would rid me of the short-term anxiety, but that is neither what I want to do nor what is best for me right now.

No matter how confident people may appear on the outside, I would hazard a guess that the vast majority of people – whether they're moving to a new area, starting at a new school, college or university, switching to become self-employed, or turning professional in their chosen area – have doubts too. One thing that separates successful people from the rest, and enables them to succeed, is their ability to embrace the unknown, knowing that, although there will be new trials, tribulations and challenges ahead, there will also be endless possibilities, new experiences and potential.

The next time you have a big life decision to make, remember this: if you wait for every possible scenario to line up and seem like the perfect opportunity, you could be stalling for a long time! For me, with this trip, I've decided what would make it successful for me. Knowing that the majority of that is within my control has enabled me to feel great about starting a new life in Asia and seeing where that takes me next.

Imagine if, as a very young child, you'd given up on learning to speak or read English because it was difficult at the time. I'm convinced that you're glad you persevered instead. I've no doubt that the same is applicable to many more areas of your life. If things don't work out exactly as you hope they will, what is the worst that could happen? Personally, I know that if things don't go to plan during my time in China, and I find that I don't want to stay, I have the means of getting myself back to England and my life there. I hope that, even if that were the case, I would have picked up some valuable life experiences along the way, and gained a better idea of what is important to me; that, even if this wasn't destined to be a fruitful next stage, I could still call it a success overall. An honest evaluation of 'what is the worst that could happen?' is often enough to get us off the ledge, ready to take a leap into the unknown.

Action: Picture one aspect of your life that is potentially scary right now. Try imagining what it could look like retrospectively, in a few years' time, if you stuck with it and allowed some of that initial discomfort to lead you in a new direction you maybe never even thought of. On a separate page, write down challenges you notice this week and try to frame these differently. Instead of 'challenges', label them 'opportunities for growth', and note what you can gain from dealing with these events. A different viewpoint will give a fresh, broader perspective on how experiences can mould you into an even better version of you. What may seem like a huge negative right now may turn out to be the biggest blessing, as your ideas about what's best for your future can so often be wrong. To help with the disappointment when it feels like nothing is going your way, try to remind yourself of a few more of these situations where things didn't play out quite to plan, but have since turned out pretty great.

Views of both sides of The Bund, lining the Huangpu river, Shanghai.

Lesson #2

You cannot spell 'reaction' without a little action

I've always wanted to help others out in life. As a result, I found that some of my happiest memories were as part of a team of volunteers working in an orphanage in Costa Rica. Being able to travel to an unknown and potentially scary environment, and perform tasks that otherwise couldn't be done, which had an impact on so many people's lives, made me feel like I was really making a difference.

These are the kind of big activities we picture when we think about being a force for good in the world. However, I also enjoy being able to put a smile on the face of somebody who is down, to help a struggling mother lift her pram up the steps, or to pass on a friendly word when needed. None of these seem like huge actions in themselves, but even something small and simple can make a huge difference in one person's life.

Today I travelled 6,000 miles across the world and was greeted at the airport by my boss-to-be and another coaching friend. As you'd hope your friends might do, they helped me with my baggage, sorted out a taxi, got me settled in and unpacked, and then we went off to dinner. My introduction to Chinese food was actually a Taiwanese restaurant, where I had some fun struggles with chopsticks, and finished off with an incredible dessert, 'Red Bean Ice', with shaved ice covered in condensed milk, red beans, pineapple and other fruits arranged in seemingly gravity-defying balance. It tasted even better than it looked.

These small actions, designed to make me feel welcome, helped me feel even better about this move. Without any of the above, this tired, bewildered Brit definitely wouldn't have started his Chinese adventure on the right foot!

Action: Try to make a little effort today, and each day this week, to do something that could make someone else smile. Not to show off, or seek public admiration, but just to chronicle each of these actions and the responses they receive as you go along. They make great points of reflection when you look back, and can really go to show just how much difference a tiny spark can make in the long-term. As one simple idea, you may never know how that smile or conversation with a stranger on the train could be potentially life changing.

Red Bean Ice – a typical Taiwanese dessert

Lesson #3

Little by little...

During the last few months I've had to get my head around a fair few unfamiliar transport systems: the subway in New York; more of London's public transport system than I'm used to; scaling a lot of Florida to catch up with friends and golf coaches, where I had to get used to driving on the wrong side of the road; and now, just two days after arriving in Shanghai, an 800-mile trip to the capital, Beijing, as a tourist.

If you look at the whole picture, the challenge of getting myself 800 miles, by train, across a strange country, where I don't yet speak the language, could definitely look like a problem; maybe even too intimidating to put myself through. Instead, I could have chosen to take the more expensive flight, with the extra hassles of air travel, or not even taken the trip at all.

But I'm here for an adventure, so challenge accepted. Now all I had to do was hail a cab, explain my destination using basic Chinese, find and collect a ticket, make it around the huge station to the notoriously prompt trains, not get in one that was going the wrong direction, and then navigate the finer details of Beijing's bustling metropolis to my hotel upon arrival. As it happened, that same task, with all its potential for disaster, actually turned out looking something like this:

- Book your ticket the day before.

- Learn Chinese words for where you want to go, write it down, and leave with lots of time to spare.

- Look at the board at the station that tells you exactly where you want to go and what time it leaves. Pretty easy, as it also has the same four digit code that your ticket shows...

- Realise you have a lot of time, go to find some lunch, and head towards the right platform.

- Go through barriers, walk down steps, get on the wrong carriage, then walk straight back off and onto the right one. Make sure you're there early, as the train leaves five minutes early.

- Sit down, get out your book and chill for the next five hours.

- Arrive in Beijing. Get off the 300 kilometres per hour train, put your subway 'journey planner' app to use, and use the touch screen (and 20p) to buy tickets for your next part of the journey.

- Look at the easy-to-follow subway map that tells you where you need to switch lines.

- Reach the subway stop, leave the station, spot the signs for your hotel, and arrive a few minutes later with quite a high level of self-satisfaction.

It really wasn't that difficult! In fact, the hardest part was deciding what to have for lunch.

Action: Big task? Important deadline? It can feel almost insurmountable if you judge yourself against the 0.1% progress you seem to be making. Instead, break that exact same momentous task into smaller pieces, work out how best to attack each individual phase, and before too long you too will find yourself travelling vast distances in whatever challenge you're facing.

Lesson #4

You ate what?!

I love travelling. I love being able to experience new environments but also, almost more than anything, I like to create memories for myself that I will look back fondly on for years to come. When I was researching life in China, one thing that constantly cropped up was how different the food would be for a Westerner. With that in mind, and wanting to test my boundaries, my first evening in Beijing, after a late arrival by train, was spent at Wángfǔjǐng night market, supposedly famous for its 'local delicacies.'

Words probably cannot do justice to quite how much of a shock my senses were in for when I arrived. The smell of something aptly named 'smelly tofu' was arguably worse than the stench of putrid rubbish in the sweltering heat and, as I looked around, I saw everything from spiders to scorpions, seahorses to fried star fish, and a host of interesting-looking fish, insects, whole ducks, and spiked fruits.

At this point, I'm sure many people would repeat the same old story in their head that there was no way they could ever buy and eat one of these strange things. However, I was there for the experience and was determined to tell myself a new story and reality: that in some cultures they would think of me as very strange for eating chicken and pork, just as I was a little perturbed by the idea of these foods. With that in mind, and with an ever-growing crowd of supporters, I chose the biggest scorpion

*Whole duck. Just one of many shocks to the Western eye from **Wángfǔjǐng** night market, Beijing*

I could, after whetting my appetite on a starter of smaller creepy crawlies.

With the camera rolling, locals clapping and cheering, and my heart beating, with my updated cultural story playing over and over in my head, I ate two large scorpions. Truthfully, they were not fantastic. Quite crunchy and with a taste of liver but, by viewing them just as food, I was able to get through these particular challenges with relatively little trouble.

I understand that eating scorpions may not be everyone's idea of fun. However, I also understand that what we tell ourselves can help shape our reality. If you continuously tell yourself that you're not worthy of a job promotion, or of the life you really want, nobody is going to convince you that you are. Instead, be very wary of what you tell yourself.

Action: For the next 24 hours, try to physically note down some of the stories you tell yourself in your head. They are exactly that – just a story – until we take action based on how we feel as a result. Often, compiling data like this and being aware of what you're currently thinking and doing can be enough to encourage you to make a change.

Lesson #5

The formula for success: fail, laugh, learn, try again, and repeat

If you want to be ultra serious, never fail, and you don't like making yourself look like a fool, then let me suggest that learning a new language is probably not the best idea for you.

During the last few days in Beijing, I have tried reading all of the metro station names, out loud, each time I've arrived at one; I have asked a friend for the Chinese word for something, and then tried to use it, in a very basic combination of words, with a stranger; and I have attempted to ask for directions and order in restaurants using a few Chinese words (followed by rather more English words!) In more than a few of these situations I have definitely not been understood, and have either had to accept failure, try again, or rely on the help of a Chinese-speaking friend to bail me out and put an end to the blank expressions staring back at me.

It would be easy to feel demoralised and give up trying; however, thinking back to the learning of ANY skill, these experiences are right in line. The first time a child walks, they stumble, yet they do not give up and decide walking is not for them. The first time you drive a car, I am sure it didn't lead to flawless gear changes and beautiful handling. Fortunately, however, you persevered, which has left you in the position you are now in – hopefully able to walk and drive, if you so desire, alongside a bunch of other learned skills.

Learning a new skill requires a lot of falling down, brushing yourself off, and starting afresh. From what I've learnt from these experiences, not only do you need to be able to accept the reality of failing constantly, you must also take pride in the small moments of success. Breaking down the seemingly insurmountable larger picture means that you can enjoy the process you are moving along, as opposed to only being satisfied at the very end. For me, the pride when I was able to ask: "where is the metro station?" and be understood (albeit by a Chinese man who also happened to speak fluent English) was SUCH a proud moment, and then gave me so much confidence to brave through the next barrage of failure, intertwined with sporadic success.

I've also learnt to differentiate between me the person, and me learning the skill. I am not a failure as a person if I pronounce a word incorrectly; I would only say I am a failure if I give up at that point. I am who I am; the action I am trying to achieve is a subsidiary part of that and shouldn't affect the mind-set that I have. After all, it's only a word.

Action: Even though it may have been a while since you learnt a new skill, and you may not like the helpless feeling of failure, it is an essential part of learning and progressing. Write down two skills you would want to learn, improve or accomplish if fear of failure was not an option. Your challenge is to start your progress on these skills with the mind-set of a child. If you fail (and you will!) just brush yourself off, start again, and be assured that this is just the start of the learning process. Nothing is learnt without a bit of failure and subsequent knowledge building at the start.

Lesson #6

Hot ass on the Great Wall of China

Today, along with a few new friends I made at the hotel, I visited the Great Wall of China. I mean, how could you possibly go to Beijing and not do this? I am not really sure what I expected, and I am rarely at a loss for words, but today...I was. I simply cannot believe that something so colossal, so high up, and so wide reaching could possibly have been built without the machinery of today. According to the locals, what was equally unbelievable was the complete lack of smog, the clear blue sky, the relatively quiet atmosphere, and the lack of tourists.

Having met these new friends the day before, we quickly decided that none of us were 'sit on the tour bus and be told what and where to do things' kind of people, so we didn't. Instead, we looked at local trains and buses, and planned our own route. This enabled us to have probably my funniest moment in China so far when, despite having a fluent Chinese speaker with us, and after a lot of confusion, Google translate told me that the dumpling I had just ordered was in fact a 'tasty bit of ass (meat!)'. It also meant that we had as much time as we wanted on the wall to take a bunch of ridiculous pictures, stage some silly videos, admire the beauty without fear of missing the bus, and then even slide down the wall on our way back down and try out some interesting new dried fruits.

After our experience of getting so close to this incredible place, I read a lot of online reviews of the various tourist trips to the wall and the general feedback was that they felt rushed, with not enough time for visitors to do what they wanted. This saddened me. After coming so far, it was almost as if many people felt their whole trip had not quite been properly fulfilled. Just a little planning on our part allowed us to have an incredible day, which turned out to be ridiculously cheap (especially as my PGA card continues to give me half price entry at most sites I visit), as well as full of laughs – once again proving, in my eyes, that money doesn't buy happiness.

Action: Next time you are faced with a tough decision, or cannot muster up the energy to take action and finish a task off, take a step back and admire. Look at how far you have come. Take note of how this next step is just like the many you've taken so far to get to this point. A lot of people I see get so far towards their dreams before the going gets a bit tough and they give up. If you've made the journey, see it out right. The easy way out may be the right option at times, but don't limit the potential of the situations you encounter by automatically choosing the easier path.

The Great Wall of China, Beijing, 21,000+ kilometres of man-made wall

CHINESE REALISATION OF THE DAY

If a supermarket says it shuts at 22:00, it doesn't. What it REALLY means is that from about 21:30 onwards they will start clearing shelves so you can no longer buy meat or dairy. It also means that when you get to the till at 21:55 (after passing countless staff playing a communal, cross-aisle game of catch) you will be the only customer still inside. As you try to leave, you will likely be locked in, have to deal with a confused security man to get let out, and then struggle to communicate to him that you are not stealing the trolley, you just need it to take your nine shopping bags to the taxi rank, and then you will return it. I'm almost tempted to try the same next week; that game of catch looked pretty fun...

CHINESE REALISATION OF THE DAY

Some Chinese people are really loud! You will never imagine just how much noise is possible when slurping noodles, unless you are there. Today, I was worried that the intensity of the guy a table away from me meant that he was somehow going to slurp the noodles off my plate too!

CHINESE REALISATION OF THE DAY

I'm on the train back to Shanghai from Beijing and suddenly my nose starts bleeding. Not just a little bit, but enough that blood now covers my face as I try to keep it from dripping on the floor. The lady next to me notices, lets out a little scream, and hands me a tissue. As I get up from my seat, I picture the toilet being a hole in the floor so quickly attempt to put on my shoes before heading out, but as blood is still dripping through the tissue and onto the floor, I just manage one shoe. Imagine the shock of the guys waiting to fill up their soup in the hot water sink, who are now waiting for a one-shoed, bloody, non-Chinese speaking guy to finish dripping blood into the sink...If I didn't already feel stared at from time to time here, now I do!

CHINESE REALISATION OF THE DAY

If you have a Chinese girlfriend, you are not their boyfriend. Instead, you are their official, unpaid photographer. Some of the guys/ handbag holders I saw in Hangzhou have the patience of saints!

City God Temple, Shanghai

Lesson #7

You are the sum of your closest friends

I knew it would happen, which makes it a lot easier, but during the settling-in stage, as I was warned, there are plenty of moments when everything feels wrong and I find myself questioning my decision to move halfway around the world. All in all, after reflection with my family, I've not done so badly. The travel; initial shopping; preparing the house to make it more like a home; the introductions to so many new people; the acclimatisation; and many other things, have all largely gone without major issues. But there are tough moments, and it's often the little things: the frustration when you fancy a healthy, comforting snack, but the dried fruits you're greeted with are nothing like you expect; discovering all the meat you eat has bones in, and almost breaking your teeth in the process; and, of course, the language barrier, which is so much more intense than you've ever experienced in any of your other travels.

It is during moments like this, however, that I have been beyond overwhelmed by the quality of people I have around me in my life. The messages from friends and family just randomly checking in on me as I settle in have been incredible, and not just from people whom I speak with regularly. I've received so many encouraging words from a variety of people who, as I reflect, I realise I have met in so many different walks of my life. When I've uncharacteristically needed to have a moan, it has been so reassuring to have people not try and 'fix me' but just listen, be there for me, maybe tell me a little joke and help me out in that way.

It reminds me of a quote that I am sure gets misquoted, rearranged and reused, but Jim Rohn (American entrepreneur, author and motivational speaker) once said: "You are the average of the five people you spend the most time with." This week has reminded me, not only that I am fortunate to have more than five people around me who I believe positively shape and influence me, but also how much the people around you really can change your life. If the five people around me had allowed me to moan, get myself into a rut, declare that I hate this move and book a return flight right away, for the home comforts of chocolate, flushable toilet paper and real milk... I simply would not be in the position I am now.

Action: Your life only has one run; there is no dress rehearsal. As tough as it may seem, make absolutely sure that the people around you are people who bring out the best in you. That does NOT mean that if you want to be a successful businessman, all your friends must also be extremely wealthy Wall Street bankers. However what I've discovered is that, despite huge contrasts in the lives of many of my friends, the ones I spend the most time with and value most highly all have an irrepressible zest for life. They all accept that there will be ups and downs during the ride and therefore they don't expend precious energy on factors beyond their control and, probably number one for me, they all smile a lot and genuinely make the world around them a better place to be. If you have people like that around you, great job, you have no action today...if not, you know what to do!

Lesson #8

Change is a process. Enjoy the journey

If you are trying to change a habit, it takes time. I deal with this every day of my working life – trying to convince people that success will not be instant, and helping them to be realistic whilst moving towards their goals. Deep down we all know this is how things work, but sometimes the desire for instant gratification and results can become too strong; we tend to only see the overall picture, which often seems very large and distant. These distant goals and aims are great, and much needed for your overall commitment. However, being able to achieve and celebrate many smaller intermediate goals along the way is what will give you the satisfaction required to continue pursuing your ultimate dream.

When I arrived in Shanghai I was hopeless at using chopsticks. I could just about manage to eat with them, but on a trip to Wagamama's would always go for the knife and fork option to save myself the embarrassment. I also knew no Chinese other than 'nĭ hăo', or how to say hello. After a few weeks here, if two of my goals had been to master those two skills, I haven't achieved either. However, from the perspective of a friend who (until today) last saw me in England, I have come on a considerable way in both of these areas. It wasn't until I realised he was impressed that I actually took the time to reflect, re-evaluate, and give myself credit. I can now eat a meal without someone feeling sorry for me and offering me a

Persistent practice eventually makes perfect – wakeboarding

fork and spoon, and I can say many more words than when I began. I am not yet at the impressive stage of being able to skilfully shell a prawn using chopsticks, or have conversations in Chinese, but I am moving forward.

As a coach, a perfectionist, and someone with a strong passion for changing the lives of others, I spend a lot of time researching, discussing, and contemplating – all to make the impact of my coaching and my life as big as possible. One area I have looked at a lot is skill acquisition and how people learn new things, whether that's a language, a golf skill set, or any other movement, pattern, or habit. One area I've focused on is random vs. blocked practice, which, in a nutshell, suggests that doing the same repeated task over and over again may lead to short-term gains and a feeling of instant success, but the levels of skill retention and actual learning are higher with scattered, random and chaotic practice.

Fun and games, team building in Zhejiang, an eastern coastal province of China

On the metro yesterday I learnt numbers 1-20 and have been going over them since, trying to solidify the knowledge. As research suggests, after a while I was able to recite all of the numbers sequentially and they seemed to flow off each other like a song. It got easy relatively quickly and could have led to a false sense of achievement if I'd let it. However, I liken it to learning a maths question. If I asked you what 17 x 7 was, the first time it may take you a while to reply correctly; but if I asked you the same question maybe 15 times, you would switch onto auto-pilot and relay 119 to me each time I asked. Is this really helping you learn a transferable skill though? Instead, later I asked a friend to call out random numbers for me to say in Chinese. It would have been easy to feel discouraged, as my speed and accuracy GREATLY dropped, however I know that this is where real learning occurs. Rather than being discouraged, I left the 'practice' feeling quite good about how this skill could be usable in real life, like for noting down someone's phone number, as opposed to the unlikely scenario of needing to count from 1-20 consecutively.

Action: Think about a challenge you're facing in your life and record in some way a simple evaluation of where you feel you are on this journey right now. Maybe write a brief sentence or take a small video or audio recording. For me, it would be a list of the Chinese words I know so far, or a short video of me attempting to use chopsticks. Then, at a designated interval – maybe a month later – add an extra checkpoint into the process so you can notice and review your new level. You will be able to see how far you have come, instead of feeling frustrated that you are not yet at the end goal, and this will give you the motivation you need to keep striving.

Embrace the feeling of failure by recognising what it is actually doing for your ability to learn. Ask yourself honestly: do I want to feel good about this skill in the short-term, or am I prepared to go through a little worthwhile pain to really develop? I've found the best way is to combine the two, enabling me to have that slight confidence boost of having learnt something, before getting stuck into the kind of practice that research has proven leads to lasting change.

CHINESE REALISATION OF THE DAY

If you want blank looks and confusion from Chinese people, ask for ¥20/£2 worth of fresh noodles at the market. I did this and the guy gave me a confused look before PILING a massive heap of noodles into a bowl on the scales. I decided I must've accidentally said ¥200/£20 as he kept going, so I pulled out a ¥20 note, to which he nodded and continued. Moral of the story: noodles are really cheap and, when we finally agreed that £2 would get me almost a year's supply, we settled on ¥2/20p worth – enough for at least a week!

CHINESE REALISATION OF THE DAY

I do not think Chinese people sweat. It has not even got close to summer humid temperatures and I am already struggling, but after watching Chinese tourists, runners, dancers, tai-chi'ers all in the street... I think they missed out on the sweating gene.

Showing the young'uns how it is done!

CHINESE REALISATION OF THE DAY

Love is all around. I just popped to the local market and then on to a little corner shop to pick up a few more things. I get the usual inquisitive looks, two of the familiar workers say hey, and we have a basic chat. Then the overly keen third one, who speaks next to no English but always tries, steps around the corner, clears her throat and recites, script-like, in near-perfect English: "Hello handsome man, I like you, do you have girlfriend or can I be please?" I'm not always the fastest thinker, but I think she may have just learnt that sentence especially and I may have picked up another admirer...I guess I'm honoured!

CHINESE REALISATION OF THE DAY

From what I've seen so far, Chinese girls spend 99.9% of their lives in high heels. This assumption is not proven yet, but I would not be surprised if required wear for a pyjama party here was PJs and heels. I've seen them worn with yoga pants, whilst walking up big hills, on a rowing boat, in the market with wet floors, and also swimming...OK, I made that last one up!

CHINESE REALISATION OF THE DAY

Black people are pretty rare in Shanghai. So I am sat with a group in a bar this evening and there happen to be two black guys, which is obviously quite confusing for all involved! I pay for a drink and stay sat down in the same seat. A few minutes later, the same lady returns to give the change back... except she goes to give it to my friend. I get her attention and watching her face, as she has to double take and realises that, hold on...there are two of you in the room, is priceless!

Lesson #9

Judging a book by its cover

Before I left for China I knew that learning Chinese was going to be one of my main goals. In order to feel like I can really 'live' somewhere, I always want to be able to communicate proficiently without having to rely on tapping phrases into my phone for a translation. I also wanted to be myself, to make Chinese friends, and to have fun and jokes with the locals. Of course, I knew this would be a long process but I was definitely up for the challenge. While still in England I had looked online for guidance, but found that many blogs and articles advised me against all this and simply described how impossible the language is to learn. Well, being a positive guy and knowing that hundreds of thousands of people, including very young kids can speak the language – I would not accept that as an excuse. So far, learning Chinese has been going quite well, but a lesson I learnt today is, I think, a definite reminder not to judge a book by its cover.

Today, I had a few moments to go over some words with my assistant. The topic was the months of the year, and pretty quickly I realised how simple this was. All I had to do was use the numbers I had already learnt and then simply add 'yuè' at the end. For example, January is translated as 'one month' or yī yuè. With a grand total of 12 numbers and one word, I was able to say all of the months of the year. Simple.

In return, we started to go over the English months... 'January...' I began, as the assistant took notes, before 'February', which at least had a similar ending. But then, as the months progressed, I realised the lunacy of it all. Each of the month names have no meaning in the English language other than being 12 random words, derived from the names of Latin emperors and gods, meant to signify the time of year. You could very easily confuse the months and be completely wrong yet have no idea, whereas after five minutes of learning the Chinese months – as long as I could remember how to count – I would never have this problem.

As I continued to go through the months in English, I realised how wrong so many people were to completely write off Chinese as an 'impossible' language. I am sure there will be plenty of tough vocabulary and ridiculous grammar rules to get my head round, but attempting this with a clear mind is much better than doing so pessimistically, with an expectation of failure. As I continued I became more aware of the difficulty of the English language. This not only gave me a whole new appreciation for those who have learnt it as their second language, but also boosted my confidence that, having already learnt to speak English, Chinese should be just as possible.

Action: There will be many beliefs that you have relayed to yourself and therefore accepted as reality. For the next day, become more attuned to your thoughts and what you are telling yourself. If you're telling yourself you cannot learn a new skill because you are 'too old' or 'don't have enough time', do you really think you will surprise yourself and achieve it? Monitor and note down these thoughts that you've been accepting as reality, and realise instead that thoughts are all they are. Once you've gained this new awareness, I'm sure it will help you along the path to rectifying what you believe you're capable of.

Lesson #10

Scooter selfies

Today was a day of many firsts: My first complete, basic conversation solely in Chinese. My first introduction to a big group of people from the local church, who I'd never met before but who had invited me to join them for some food and games. My first time being able to help someone else out with directions for the metro. My first ride on a Chinese scooter – although I'm still not sure if this is a legal taxi or not!

All of these 'firsts' turned out to be great things, which went well, but in more than one of them there was definitely potential to feel scared and avoid taking action.

In my first few weeks, I have taken the 25-minute walk to the nearest metro station a few times. The first time, I wanted to check out the distance and timings, after which I knew it was quite a way, and not the safest of roads to walk. Constant building work, houses being knocked down, burst water pipes, and the many other calamities of a growing area, do not make for the most tranquil of walks – not to mention the fact that the 'path' seems to merge with the road far too readily for comfort!

The next few times, I made myself late for things, faced that risky walk, and got a bit sweaty – mainly because I didn't know how to order a taxi and didn't trust the scooters that whizzed by. Today however, coming home at nearly midnight, I decided enough was enough and finally did what my logic had been telling me for a few days. I spoke some basic Chinese, managed to scope out the driver of the least worn out scooter (or at least, the one with the fewest signs of bungled gaffer tape repairs!), negotiated a price, and was on my way. A few minutes, some funny pictures, and one 'jumped' red light later, and I was back home – all for a fare equivalent to just £1. I could have kept convincing myself that my way was best, even though I knew it wasn't, but instead I chose to make the change and, as a result, made things a whole lot easier for myself.

Action: In what instances in your life are you aware of that a change is needed? Deep down you know that this is the right change, and yet making that first move is scary. Fast-forward a year and picture yourself in that same situation if you take no action now. Next, picture yourself as having taken action and see how much further it could get you. Luckily, when we quieten down our minds, and slow down enough to listen to our own intellect, we can come up with some great wisdom and insights. Give it a go, trust yourself on these decisions, and make the choice you know is right for you.

Rows upon rows of often non road-worthy scooters

Lesson #11

Change the focus of the picture you're taking

One of the things I was jokingly warned about before coming to China was that looking different to 'the norm' would likely make me the subject of many stares, points, and photo requests – as well as sneaky, candid photos. I was told this would happen in all kinds of situations, from work and the supermarkets, to subways and tourist attractions, and many more.

Well, I'm still just a couple of weeks in and can safely say the friend who told me this was definitely not wrong. I've managed to make light of these weird situations numerous times so far, by quickly whipping my own camera out and snapping them right back, or pulling crazy faces, and even pointing back right at them. This often gets a bewildered look, before we mutually laugh at the surrealism of the situation.

It's still early days for me, but many people have told me how annoying this can get in the long-run and I'm determined to not let that happen. In fact, today's events made me sure it never will.

I spent the day visiting Suzhou, where I filled my morning negotiating trains, visiting the city's numerous parks, gardens and pagodas as well as posing for silly pictures – with a lot of walking and getting lost in between! I even found a bit of home comfort in the form of that great British export, a Marks and Spencer's store, before deciding it was time for lunch. I chose a clean-looking fast-food restaurant, where I ordered a beef noodle dish and picked up some spicy duck intestines too, which caught my eye and actually tasted great. As I went to order, I realised that all ten or so members of staff had suddenly stopped working and were stood watching me intently. We all shared a giggle about my broken Chinese as I counted out my money, and then I went to take my seat.

My chopstick-using, noodle-eating technique can't have been up to scratch because several times I looked up and noticed a worker attempting to disguise their laughter by looking away from me! Being the subject of so much attention whilst eating was almost a bit strange until, out of nowhere, another worker said in perfect English, "here you go sir" and handed me a napkin. As I thanked him, I knocked a chopstick off the table, onto the floor, and he rushed off to bring me another one. Less than a minute later, he returned again with a friend from a neighbouring restaurant, who spoke a bit of English. We had a very basic conversation, where he asked my name, where I was from, and so on.

Then all of a sudden it hit me: all the other people who had been watching, staring, and taking pictures of me all day are just human beings like me, who are interested in other people. They aren't rude, just intrigued by something different, and if language wasn't an issue I'm sure they would love to chat and find out a bit about our similarities and differences! I finished up my meal, practised my best Chinese by saying thanks and "great food" to a few of the staff and, in return, received huge smiles and a really warm feeling.

Action: Often it is easy to only see your own point of view and base your reactions on that. Next time someone acts in a way that seems 'off' to you, stop and have a think. Instead of jumping to conclusions about what you perceive their actions, tone or response may imply, imagine an alternative. Take a moment to practise empathy and think of scenarios that may have influenced the way they responded, instead of just reacting negatively. This week, try and note down three different ways you could perceive a particular situation from your day. That same congested car journey could make you hugely angry, and cause you to act on that anger, or it could give you some quiet time to pay attention to areas of your life that need work, or listen to music that makes you smile. An angry glare from a stranger could leave you feeling irritated and offended, or it could be an opportunity to share a smile that might brighten up their stressful day. That very same situation can be viewed in many different ways; some are much more productive than others and can lead to lots of positive knock-on effects.

Snap!

A trip back to London complete with a great friend's wedding and customary selfie!

Lesson #12

Trust and let it go

Shanghai ERA Intersection of Time acrobatics show, rated #2 on TripAdvisor for attractions, was something that made me experience many different emotions. Anxiety and fear for the performers; confusion, disbelief, and awe; wonder, shock, and more. The acts were seriously impressive, but what made the whole thing even more surreal was the lack of safety equipment and, consequently, my acute awareness that, if anything were to go wrong, it would likely go very wrong indeed.

The range of acts was astonishing: a man balancing on an uneven board whilst launching bowls into the air and catching them on his head; eight motorcyclists whizzing around, chasing each other in a sphere hardly big enough to contain them; men jumping over skipping ropes while balancing atop a rotating drum, a staggering 25 feet up in the air; stilt wearers being launched way up into the air by a seesaw-like catapult; acrobats diving through rings up to ten feet high; multiple women just appearing out of a pot; and, finally, a man flinging a china vase into the air before catching it on his head, spinning it around, and performing some really incredible feats, all the while keeping his fragile prop intact.

So many of the acts seemed to defy possibility and I was really impressed, however what really got me was the trampolinists. Whereas two of them were performing on a regular trampoline, one had just a piece of cloth acting as her trampoline. As she soared into the air her landing surface was not even stable; the people holding it moved around to try and help her land on the thin strip of material. What struck me was how much harder this must be as, instead of your success being solely down to you, she now also had to trust in others.

As I tried to imagine what she was thinking, I recalled the thoughts and feelings I'd gone through when I did my first bungee jump, or when I decided that falling out of a plane at 18,000 feet was a good idea. The risk is always there, but you have to trust in the knowledge that you should be safe. You can spend all day looking at statistics – tandem skydiving recently reported a safety record of 0.003 student fatalities per 1,000 jumps in the last 10 years, therefore making death by lightning or being stung by a bee much more likely – however, simply reading and taking on board these facts won't necessarily result in you taking action.

The trampolinist appeared to have complete trust in those around her and, even though she must have had plenty of falls throughout her training and life, she had likely pushed these to the back of her mind, allowing her to give this – the most important thing right now – her full attention. As a result, her elegance and skill definitely grabbed mine.

Action: I've been told a few times, as I've progressed through my career, that a feeling of not being ready for the next job you're offered is a great thing. It means that you can develop into it, rather than already being capable of everything it entails and therefore not having the chance to grow. This story reminded me of that advice. Prepare fully so that you can feel confident in what you do, and then let go, trust in the abilities that you have developed, get out there, and show the world what you are capable of doing and how awesome you are.

CHINESE REALISATION OF THE DAY

Sometimes, despite your best efforts, you just cannot hold in your laughter, and this is probably my funniest sight so far in China. It is evening and a young lady, clearly in a rush for the metro, heels and all, rushes towards the barrier. She gets out her card to swipe through and is already pushing through the barrier, except for the fact her card has not swiped. Instead of seamlessly gliding through, only her top half does as the barrier clatters her legs. At the speed she was going, she almost does a full flip as she lands on her back. Fortunately, despite quite a hard fall she is not hurt apart from her pride. On the plus side, she made it through the barrier without paying, so likely saved herself a cheeky 40p!

CHINESE REALISATION OF THE DAY

The selfie craze has hit here. The strange thing though is watching people posing for them, but always the wrong way. There is always a monument, attraction, or picture-worthy item in front, but the selfie just has a bush, path or concrete pillar in the background.

CHINESE REALISATION OF THE DAY

If you want to get approving glances on the metro, casually catch the stray mosquito in one hand as you text with the other. Act like your skills are perfectly normal and that you're not even surprised at yourself. Let the mosquito fall from your hand onto your trouser leg just to prove you got it, casually push it on to the floor and act like nothing happened. For additional dramatic effect, don't look up at the approving glances from everyone around who had been flapping it away; just play it cool...!

CHINESE REALISATION OF THE DAY

Despite what people will try and tell you about the Chinese and their lack of queuing skills, my evidence is proving they are often wrong. More than a few times this week, I've seen teenagers and young kids willingly give up their seats for random mothers, I've seen gentlemanly old Chinese men allow others to sit before them, and middle aged men arguing hard as they insist that somebody else deserves a place more than them. Manners are so great to watch!

CHINESE REALISATION OF THE DAY

Once in a while, your scooter taxi driver back from the metro station will think he is Lewis Hamilton. This is not a bad thing if you're in a rush to get home. However, it is a bad thing if the roads aren't flat; you have both hands full, carrying gifts from England that your parents have sent over; the scooter seat has no grip, so you find yourself getting uncomfortably cosy with the driver in front of you; and the driver definitely does not have the driving skills of Lewis Hamilton...

How to use a toilet...

Lesson #13

Everything will work out OK in the end; if things aren't OK, it isn't the end

As I was warned, bad things seem to happen in multiples when you're abroad and away from home comforts, almost as if life is testing you to see how strong you really are in the face of adversity. These last few days have been another test for me but I am happy to say that, on the whole, I have come out pretty well and been able to learn some lessons myself.

Today I've felt a bit frustrated that I haven't been teaching as many golf lessons as I'm used to. In the midst of this frustration, as I started to question myself, I stopped and tried to step outside of the situation, to take a more objective view. It would have been very easy to feel sorry for myself, complain that I knew it was never a good idea to move here, and dig myself into a hole.

Instead, I looked at the fact that in my first few months, helped by the fact I've had fewer lessons to teach, I've:

- Not had to turn down many social plans, which has helped me to make some great friends

- Spent a lot of time training the assistants on how to use the technology we have, and also preparing lesson reviews

- Got myself up to scratch on a number of technologies I don't have as much experience with

- Been able to pester anybody and everybody to help me learn more and more Chinese

How many Chinese people does it take to understand a foreigner?

- Had time to myself to reflect and evaluate my progress as I settle into a completely new world

Instead of getting angry at the current situation, I had to see the problem as a story in motion, not yet completed. As I write this, I am still not any busier with lessons but I imagine that, when I am, I will be very grateful for the time I had to do all these other things at the beginning of my time here.

Action: Have a look through your life at a tricky situation you are in. Instead of seeing the pain and frustration of the current situation, try to imagine where you are currently as the middle point of the 'story.' Maybe the perseverance that you are developing will stand you in good stead for a future, bigger task; maybe the humility required is essential for your personal growth. I am sure you know that we learn best through making mistakes and learning from them, and that nothing would change if, on a daily basis, we only experienced successes. Today, try to take pride in your failures and joy in the characteristics you're developing in the face of your struggles, remembering that: "everything will work out OK in the end; if things aren't OK, it isn't the end."

Lesson #14

The mirror can lie... What you see isn't always what you get

So far I love the challenge of learning Chinese. Although not quite as difficult as I anticipated, this language does have the uncanny ability to make you feel like you have a memory of approximately two seconds. Due to the completely different sounds used, you can hear a word, repeat it a few times and then, just moments later, attempt to recall it and find yourself completely lost. If you're afraid of feeling silly and incompetent, Chinese may not be for you.

I've just got home from a bar, where I went out with a small group of friends, and ended up meeting three French girls and playing cards for almost three hours. If you're thinking, "who plays cards in a bar?" then we're on the same page. That was my first comment, and then three hours seemed to pass...

During the night I tried out my almost forgotten GCSE level French and was pleasantly surprised. In the last few years I've only used it sporadically, while teaching golf on a cruise ship, but I'm sure my ability to communicate (although definitely not grammatically correctly!) has improved. As a result, the girls kept telling me how good I was – even though, realistically, their English was pretty much flawless. We then got onto speaking a bit of Chinese and, strangely, I found I was helping them out with some words and tones, despite having been here for a fraction of the time they have – leading them to conclude that I was some kind of language guru. Now, even though I'm sometimes quite confident, I'm also realistic and would never label myself that, especially in comparison to their almost flawless speech.

This reminded me though of the limits we sometimes put on ourselves, from experience or pre-conceived ideas. These girls had only known me for a few hours and based their judgment of my language skills on that. For me to hold the same elevated view of my own skills would probably take gaining fluency in another five languages, and even then it would be easy to dismiss my skills as unimpressive, or compare myself to someone who can speak even more languages. We can always find ways to go on striving for something unattainable. These girls, seeing me for just a snapshot moment in my life, were able to give an honest opinion, which was surprising and great to hear.

Action: Especially in China, it is very common to brush off compliments; refusing to accept them is part of their culture. My challenge for you today is this: whenever you are complimented, accept it graciously and also make an effort to dish out compliments when they're deserved. Even though I thought it was obvious, and they weren't fishing for compliments, the girls were genuinely overwhelmed when I let them know their English was great. I'd assumed the fact we could converse with no problems at all would give that away, but maybe not! In the same way, their compliments on my French were genuine and pure, not comparing me to a French friend, or to themselves, just an honest reflection of what they had seen. Genuine compliments can change moments, days, weeks, or even lives, so get out there and tell some people what you really think.

Lesson #15

Standing out from the crowd

I've never been a huge Formula 1 fan, largely because I didn't understand it. To my untrained eye, the guy with the fastest car always won, and there wasn't much skill or action involved, other than maybe during the first lap. Fast forward a few years and I had met Lewis Hamilton a few times, when he played at my local golf course; I'd helped Damon Hill a little with his golf; and been on a few trips to Monaco, where I got to see the impressive street circuit. I wouldn't say I was hooked but, when I found out the F1 was coming to Shanghai, I had to get tickets.

After the tickets were bought, the waiting was over, and we'd taken our seats, I still expected 56 laps of watching cars whizz by to get samey after the initial few. How wrong I was. I absolutely loved it and was on my feet for pretty much the whole race. Not only was the sound incredible, the manoeuvres and speeds on the turn were seriously impressive – much more than I'd imagined they could be. To add to that, local boy Lewis Hamilton led for the whole race and did my home county of Hertfordshire proud!

After the race we noticed a few people had managed to get to the other side of some large fences and onto the track. Looking around for a while, we saw how this was done. Scaling a 12-foot wall, followed by a pretty big jump down, meant that a few minutes later we too were on the track where the race had been taking place just moments prior. As we made our way towards the start line, the atmosphere was incredible; we saw Niki Lauda giving an interview, the cars being returned to their garages, and teams of mechanics still busy working in their areas. A few drivers were milling about, as well as the fellow daredevil spectators who had made it to the track. Everywhere I looked there were spectators taking selfies on the track and it made me think: I've never been one to fit the mould, and I always want to do something different and memorable instead of joining the crowd. So I did…

Instead of the standard pictures I saw everybody else taking, I did what I always do and tried to create an exciting picture that I would look back on and be able to laugh at myself for – in addition to doing 25 push-ups on the start line, as inspired by Milo, an American coaching friend of mine. It was a lot of fun, and definitely memorable, but it was an encounter on the metro home that really inspired this story. I got chatting to a Belgian couple who were wearing F1 hats and, as we talked, they looked through my pictures. The wife kept commenting on how incredible my pictures were and how much fun it looked like I'd had. We had both been at the same event but, by working out how to get on to the track, and with a bit of creativity and stupidity, I was left with some priceless pictures and memories while, by the sounds of it, she was left feeling a bit disappointed.

Action: This is the one and only chance you get at life on earth. Following the path of what 'should be done' is dull. Go out and blaze your own trail, not limited by what others have done before you, because you are unique and awesome in your own way. This week, attempt to think outside the box a little more and see what is possible for you to achieve.

Lesson #16

Reflecting on a short life, well lived so far

Sometimes, despite the ease of communication nowadays – thanks to Skype calls, FaceTime, WhatsApp and Facebook messages, multiple notifications, likes, pokes and tweets – living 6,000 miles away from those closest to you can feel exactly that: a really long way. Especially after years of living and working around the world, the distance becomes increasingly challenging, as the idea of 'home' grows vaguer, and you always seem to be away and missing people. However, I know that is the price you pay for having a rich life of travel, and I wouldn't change it for the world.

Today, when feeling furthest from home, I did a few things to remind myself of some fantastic memories. I started by putting the 5,000 songs from my music collection into one playlist and playing them on random. I couldn't believe how many of them brought back happy memories of the moments in life that they've accompanied. It brought me back to times with special people in my life – family, life on the cruise ship, fresher's year at uni, the end of exam season, my uni housemates, family holidays growing up, golf practice sessions, my church family, drumming gigs, summers abroad, and so many other happy times.

While these songs played, I looked through photos and attempted to pick out 50 special ones that brought back special memories. A fair few hours later, with over 200 pictures chosen, I had made up a few collages, full of life events, ready to print and frame for my wall. As I looked back at the many people I've encountered along my journey, I instantly felt a whole lot less alone. Despite not speaking to them all on a daily or even regular basis, all of these people have enriched my life and I am very grateful for it.

Knowing, retrospectively, that so many of those situations – where I had started off in the unknown, and relatively alone – had actually all worked out very well, gave me a great insight into my present position. It is very easy to forget how blessed you are and bemoan negative situations. Looking back, I was overwhelmed by all the people who I can call friends, and all the memories I've made up till now. It certainly gave me renewed strength to carry on living out this latest phase of life with all that I have, knowing that in a few years I will be able to look back on yet another fantastic chapter of my life.

Later, as I waited for my metro, I sent a few random WhatsApp voice messages to friends dotted around the globe who I hadn't spoken to for a while. Of course, I was genuinely interested in hearing from them but was amazed at what came back to me, and how happy I was to hear their voices. People were delighted to know I was thinking of them, and I was able to hear so many pieces of great news from them, as well as being able to connect with them and understand their current challenges.

In a crowded metro, I was literally crying with laughter as I heard from a friend who had just had braces put in; I felt immensely proud as a friend told me she'd been recommended to pass the first year of teacher training; and I felt so special as a few of my best friends told me of their plans to come and see me later in the year. All of these friendships are ones I have put a lot of time into at different stages of my life, and I was so grateful to be able to touch base with all these incredible people; to feel as if I was there, with them. In our increasingly busy lives, it is great to be able to appreciate those who have helped you, through their words and actions, and who've been there for many adventures, calamities, and other experiences.

Action: Set aside 30 minutes before you go to bed this evening to be grateful for things in your life, to revisit forgotten areas of your past, and be thankful for how all of these situations have enabled you to develop into the fantastic person you are today. Browse through some old photographs, call up a friend you've lost contact with, send a handwritten letter to a mentor, and listen to some songs that mean something to you, or simply sit and imagine. Never underestimate how big a difference it can make, or how valued you can make someone feel, when you reach out with gratitude. Challenge yourself to become that person who's known for making others feel appreciated.

A hug from an elephant is not something that happens every day!

CHINESE REALISATION OF THE DAY

Likely in attempt not to lose 'face', a Chinese person will always help you with directions or any other question you may have, even if realistically they have absolutely no clue. When asking at the metro station today whether the next train took the up or down loop of the line, the first guy told me that this particular train had finished running for the night and pointed at his watch, whereas the next guy told me it was the third train that would be right (30 minutes away). Both seemed 110% sure of their advice... I got on the first train and took a quick peek as it pulled in, and the view of the map and flashing light clearly told me this train would get me where I wanted! It is this same logic that means on another occasion I was told the direction I wanted was North, South, East AND West, depending on who I asked!

CHINESE REALISATION OF THE DAY

On the metro, you will always experience some funny moments. Today I thought it started well, as I got on and saw the stunt double of Michael McIntyre, only Chinese! It then got better as a Chinese man came and shook my hand, saying "Obama, Obama!" However, nothing could have prepared me for walking out of my station and realising today must be some kind of comic book day at the convention centre. As I stepped out, the first thing I saw was at least 50 people in all kinds of outfits – multi-coloured hair, people acting as dogs on chains, superheroes, and so much more. NEVER a dull moment!

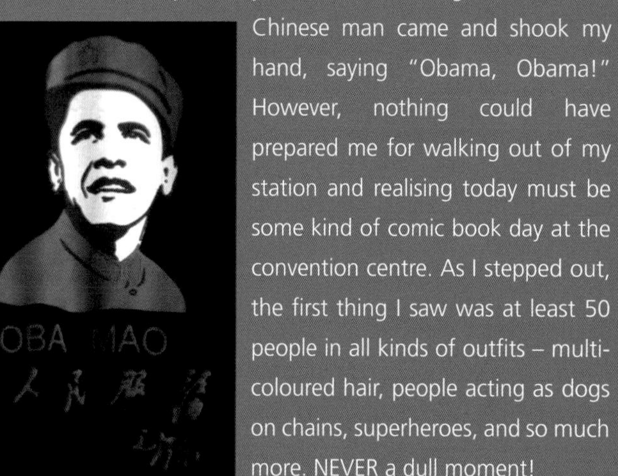

CHINESE REALISATION OF THE DAY

There must be a serious shortcoming in the amount of black actors, celebrities and sports people seen in Chinese media. The number of times I've been called Obama, or asked if I am his son or brother, is frankly ridiculous. Today I answered yes... that sure confused them and put an end to the jokey look on their face!

CHINESE REALISATION OF THE DAY

China can cause very quick changes in your mood and thoughts. Yesterday it rapidly went from compassion to absolute disbelief, as I let an 80-year-old lady barge past me onto the elevator as she was holding a very young kid and then, half way up, she went and spat over the side of the elevator, where (out of view, but still there) people were waiting to get on to the same escalator! Today it was anger, turned to relief and joy, as I realised my front door was ajar because I had asked my landlord to come in and fix my new air con, and not because I'd been burgled. It then turned to slight annoyance when I realised the worker hadn't taken his shoes off and I now have his footprints all over my house, including right next to my fridge... maybe he got peckish!

CHINESE REALISATION OF THE DAY

Chinese people walk into the metro station with their arms swinging quite wildly back and forth. They also walk in close proximity to each other, especially during the rush hour times. This means that unless you are very careful (or, in my case, fortunate because she JUST missed) you may lose the ability to create children in the future.

Lesson #17

Act first, think later

Picture the best meal you've ever had. Thick, juicy steak, crisp on the outside and pink in the middle; every type of deliciously fresh seafood imaginable, both raw and cooked, combined with endless, perfectly blended flavours and smells; add in some Chinese soup dishes; vegetables so tasty they could almost turn meat-loving me into a vegetarian; then throw in expensive traditional Chinese spirits and limited edition beers. Once you've imagined all of that, double the level of deliciousness and you may just have come close to at least one of the gastronomic sensations I was fortunate enough to have just encountered.

The location: the restaurant owned by one of the golfers who comes to the academy

The occasion: none in particular

The language exclusively spoken: Chinese, with a large dose of universal humour and gesturing

How close I came to saying no: very

I was first told about this meal during the day, by one of the assistants, but in very broken English, and I was a bit confused. Fast forward a few hours and I had pretty much decided I wouldn't go. I didn't know who else would be going, it was raining, I was tired, and I had a million and one other excuses. The main reason though was feeling like I wouldn't be able to communicate, which is a particular challenge for me right now. As you've probably already realised, I'm not one to be intimidated or put off by challenges, but the idea of sitting there mute for a few hours wasn't high up my priority list. However, I was eventually convinced; the driver turned up, and I got in, with absolutely no idea where I was going.

A few hours later and I have experienced incredible food; deepening of relationships; countless jokes and hilarious moments, all through our combined attempts at basic Chinese and English; crazy Chinese drinking games. Plus, all in all, no awkwardness or miscommunications.

So what changed my mind? Asking myself: what is the worst that could happen?

In retrospect, of course, this was a great decision and I would have been stupid to say no. At the time though, it felt like a viable option. Asking myself this question forced me to play out the situation and realise that, despite the language barrier, I'm pretty expressive and able to communicate without words; I'd been invited to this event so was obviously wanted there and wouldn't be ignored; and I can also speak enough basic Chinese to get by. All of that was enough to convince me and, other than the food baby I am currently sporting, I would say it was a pretty awesome decision.

Action: In an area of your life where you feel change is needed, but that change is scary, play the situation out in your head and determine what would be the worst-case scenario if everything went wrong. If your experiences are anything like mine, you will be pleasantly surprised that what you expect to be potentially earth-shattering consequences are actually often as small as perhaps a little embarrassment or loss, but the potential reward is far, far greater if you just take that leap.

Lesson #18

Smiling is a universal language

One of the things I've found most frustrating about not being able to communicate fully in Chinese is not being able to share laughs and silliness with those around me. Often I have got into a taxi, or joined a queue at the supermarket, and just wanted to make a silly little joke or comment and bring a smile to the face of someone I've just met. In a language that has very few similarities with my own, and in which I am progressing slowly, this has been frustratingly difficult at times.

The good news: smiling and laughter are a universal language that can be used instantly to simply bring people together, improve moods, and create special moments.

Today I took a taxi to where I was meeting a friend for dinner. This started amusingly when the text I had for the address was too small for the taxi driver to read and he got quite confused. He pretended to know where he was going, but I knew he was unsure. As I couldn't zoom in on the picture, I thought it would be a good idea to use his phone to take a picture, zoom in on that and make it legible. This process, with limited Chinese, was quite amusing, resulting in him deciding to show me a fair few of the pictures stored on his phone, including cartoon characters, family members and friends. Somehow he also misinterpreted my gestures as a request for him to take a selfie with me, so that was attempted as well before, eventually, I got my point across. When he could then zoom into the picture and read the address he absolutely howled with laughter, uncontrollably loud. As he read out the street number I'd been saying to him just moments earlier, there was a really special moment of mutual understanding after minutes of confusion. Despite not being able to communicate through words, there was no way we could have had a deeper connection; such was the power of laughter.

Just to make things even more random, after a few moments of silence, as I checked a separate message on my phone, I was interrupted by the taxi driver again laughing loudly. He then pulled a picture out of his wallet, presented it to me, and told me that I was President Obama! I'm not sure where this came from, but it gave us both a good laugh, reminded me of the randomness of some Chinese people, and was another uplifting moment, full of joy, from such a simple and silly event. I got out of the taxi and, although I was already in a typical good mood, I felt even better and more refreshed, just thanks to a few moments of madness and smiles with a complete stranger.

Action: No matter if you're having a great or even a terrible day, set yourself the challenge of being present in the moment and finding something around you that can make you smile. Maybe it's the clean air you're breathing in, the fact you're healthy and have people who care for you, or the comforting smell of fresh washing. Whatever it is, allow yourself to smile, beam or, better still, let out a full laugh.

Lesson #19

Missing the bus

This evening I ate dinner in the best sushi restaurant I've ever visited. The food was absolutely incredible, and there was something really welcoming about the tradition of leaving your shoes at the door as you went in to be shown to your table. Plate after plate of the finest cuts of salmon, tuna, squid, shrimp and beef kept appearing – in between which I discovered that eating avocado with chopsticks is no mean feat!

We finished the meal and I went to catch the metro to meet a new friend in the city. I had to travel further away from her to change onto the right line, but the journey was only a few stops so I wasn't too worried. Unfortunately, I became so engrossed in what was going on around me – a teenager obliviously walking into a pole whilst texting, a child almost being allowed to drop their pants and use the train as a toilet, and an unbelievable public display of affection by the middle-aged couple in the carriage next to me – that I missed my stop. This in itself shouldn't have been a problem, except that missing my stop meant the train had taken the lower of the two potential routes and getting back wasn't going to be easy. When I stepped onto the platform, I realised I had missed the last train in the opposite direction by two minutes!

I used my basic language skills to ask the metro workers how I could get back onto the right line and was pointed in the general direction of the bus stop a couple of hundred metres (and several corners) away. I made my way out of the station and, after asking two locals "bus, where is?" in Chinese, found myself at the bus stop, where unfortunately I was confronted by a sign with absolutely zero Pinyin or English names or times, only Chinese characters. I asked the one other person there for help but he didn't know where my stop was and I suddenly felt a bit concerned, not least because his tone seemed slightly off.

How wrong I was.

Less than ten seconds later, he was on the phone and I recognised him saying the station name I had just asked him about. I also recognised him asking if his friend could speak English, but then the conversation ended. He immediately made another phone call to a friend who, it turned out, was able to speak English and translate the information that the previous friend had provided.

This complete stranger had just made two phone calls to try and help me get on the right bus and make my journey easier. I was touched. As my bus pulled in, he pointed me onto it and then had a word with the driver. A few stops later, the bus driver looked at me, pointed, and I had indeed arrived at where I needed to be, hugely relieved. I went on to meet my friend right on time and had a great evening, having had a much richer experience than if I hadn't missed my stop on the metro.

Action: It doesn't have to be a huge action at all, but today try and challenge yourself to donate a bit of your time, money, or effort to help somebody else out in need. Make someone feel valued by making an effort to help them out in any small way, and I guarantee you will feel a great sense of achievement – as well as positively influencing their experience too.

Lesson #20

Human interaction wins the day

On my days off I always want to explore a new place, to make some new memories, and to experience something I haven't done before. The idea of fitting into a routine doesn't appeal to me and, knowing how much variety there is around me, I shouldn't find this too hard. However, the evening before my most recent day off, the friend with whom I was due to visit a nearby town the following morning was called in to cover a co-worker and, although he was very apologetic, our plans disappeared just like that. I was then left with two options: make the same train journey alone, or meet up with a new friend, who was only free until around 3pm and therefore had to stay within Shanghai.

I went for option two, and I'm very glad I did. Although I don't mind spending time in my own company – and, in fact, did a lot of this in my practice and development as a golfer – this second option was definitely better.

After crossing the city on the metro and trying to spot each other at the agreed metro station, we spent the morning wandering around Pudong, in awe at how much bigger the buildings are when you're stood at the base of them. We went into the Shanghai World Financial Centre, where we saw the model of The Bund area and realised just how much of it we had both left unexplored so far. We laughed at the cute little sniffer dogs, which looked the complete opposite of intimidating, and then made our way high up into the sky to the observation area. We made conversation with an American woman, who had been here for a few months seeing her daughter, and who gave us a dinner recommendation. We borrowed chopsticks and took some really silly but memorable pictures as we looked down on the city below. We saw many new sights that we decided were going to have to be explored soon, and tried to pinpoint exactly where we lived. We photobombed a few pictures, laughed at a few Chinese boyfriends/bag carriers/official full time photographers and, all in all, had a great time chatting about our lives and our reasons for being in Shanghai. We went back down the tower and took some more pictures, before eating some fantastic teppanyaki food and going our separate ways – her to work, and me to carry on checking out the area.

There is something so invigorating about human interaction, something that made my day fantastic, despite missing out on visiting somewhere new. There will be plenty of time for that, but the opportunity to laugh, explore, discover, and be with somebody else was priceless.

Action: Maybe it could be an old friend, an ex-colleague, family member, or university friend; whoever it is, take the time today to send someone a text, Facebook message or email – or, even better, call, Skype or FaceTime them. Life is so much richer when you can share your memories with other people. It is well worth spending the time to let somebody know exactly how much they mean to you and how much you enjoy their company.

CHINESE REALISATION OF THE DAY

If you forget a Chinese word and try to translate it for the father of your student during their lesson, make sure you get the right word. Fat fingers and trying to find the word 'shot' leads to a quick scramble to erase the findings and a confused look: "Just hit one more canine excrement please..."

CHINESE REALISATION OF THE DAY

Driving is different here. So, our driver today tries getting up a steep hill by the hotel in third gear and, of course, stalls. He then doesn't turn on the ignition but, instead, puts the clutch down, starts rolling backwards and swerving all over the place, doesn't brake, and then crashes at about 20mph into the car behind, A little back pain but fortunately there was a car there or we would have smashed into a concrete pillar and then into the water... With the next driver, we made it on safely to our rural destination for a traditional Chinese seasonal ritual, where we ate in a restaurant, drank Baiju, tasted all of the possible cuts of the lamb and now, according to Chinese beliefs, will never be cold in winter!

CHINESE REALISATION OF THE DAY

Apparently, at 24, I am way too old to be single here in China. Despite absolutely loving my current relationship situation and meeting lots of fun people, barely a week goes past where a student isn't trying to set me up with a beautiful, funny, wealthy friend or co-worker. The fact that I am the same age AND born in the same year (!) means I should be a perfect match for the woman I'm set up with tomorrow apparently.

CHINESE REALISATION OF THE DAY

Don't jump to conclusions. A student's mum today asked if her young, committed and promising golfing daughter could become like me when she is older. Thinking she was wondering if she could be a professional golfer, I replied that she already has a head start on me, as she has started a lot younger. My little feeling of pride that I had inspired her quickly turned to embarrassment when it turned out she wanted to know if her daughter would grow to have a physique like mine from just playing golf. She told me it looks great on me, but not so great for her daughter!

What happens if you don't use the brake!

Lesson #21

Stepping out of your comfort zone

Today I went to visit a friend in Suzhou, a 30 minute train ride west of Shanghai, full of canals, gardens, peace and quiet. I say 30 minutes, but if you miss your train and end up taking the slow train, it's more like an hour – as I discovered! I was also slightly disconcerted, having bought my ticket for about 25% of the normal price, when I realised that getting to my carriage involved walking past several carriages full of beds. I genuinely imagined that I had somehow booked myself onto a train that would take 12 hours to arrive, so I stopped a member of staff, who pulled off her hat, brought out a train timetable from underneath and confirmed that it was, in fact, the one hour journey I'd been expecting. With my confidence renewed, I boarded the train.

As I'd booked my ticket late, there were no first class tickets left. Unlike in the UK, a first class ticket really is advisable unless you don't mind the very cramped, often noisy, and slightly smelly conditions of the carriages often used by people making long and slow trips back to their hometowns or to visit family around the country. As I made my way to my carriage, it was pretty cramped and I was, of course, the only non-Chinese person there. The stares and confused glances only got worse as I decided I was going to make the most of the situation and, after finding my seat and getting my phrase book and iPad out, started trying to converse with the people at my table.

What happened over the next hour was almost non-stop Chinese conversation, despite almost every other word needing to be checked in my phrasebook before being regurgitated. I managed to speak enough Chinese to explain my job and how long I had been here; discuss with my newfound friends what our favourite beers were; tell them I was going home in March for the wedding of one of my best friends; and, finally, discover that the journey the family were on was going to take them nine hours, so they wouldn't arrive until 5am. For someone who only speaks limited bits of the language, it was so fulfilling and fun to see the interest this discussion generated. Many of the people nearby were stopping in to hear our 'conversations' and, just through the power of gesturing and some words, it turned into an hour full of jokes, friendship and fun times.

A message from my brother later on made it feel all the more rewarding. As I relayed the story he told me how proud he was. He recalled a trip to France several years earlier, after I had been studying French for a while, when I'd not been prepared to step out of my comfort zone and, as a result, was barely able to communicate. I'm glad to see that a lot has changed.

Action: Comfort zones are exactly that: comfortable. However, real growth, opportunity and unexpected situations rarely occur when we are in our comfort zones. Today, when you are faced with a situation with a safe option and also a potentially beneficial yet unnerving option, give the second one a thought. Looking back, I would not have traded this experience for the world, and I so easily could have missed out on it if I'd just stuck my headphones in and sat in silence for the whole hour. The world is full of fantastic people, situations and opportunities; do your best today to find some of those.

Lesson #22

Stop and smell the roses

If you go up some of the tallest towers in Shanghai, in almost every direction you will see a multitude of other towers, minimal open space, and the spectacular results of many architects competing to build the most visually appealing buildings possible. You will also see helipads, tennis courts and swimming pools on roofs, and ant-like people walking around seemingly aimlessly below. From such a height it is incredible to be looking down onto almost all the other large towers on the Pudong side of the river and, in terms of gaining awareness of the vast expanse of the city, I don't think there are many better ways. During this time, however, I was pretty surprised to see, not far from the foot of the Shanghai World Finance Centre building I was in, a large open space that was half grass and half water, so I had to go and check it out.

I made my way back down the tower and headed straight towards this park area. In an area of Shanghai that's so lively, hardworking and professional, this patch of nature definitely stood out against its backdrop of corporate towers, stretching high into the air, where many workers were slaving away at their desks. This encounter, so seemingly out of place, taught me a very powerful lesson. As I looked around, I saw young families, older couples, and just a handful of men and women in suits, who I assumed were from the offices nearby. The most striking image though, which I wish I could have captured, was of four men in business suits, sat on the ground with their shoes off, watching the world go by. It would be impossible to guess, but from their dress code I imagined this moment of tranquillity was a world away from the manic situation their work life involved. They were just taking the time to stop, metaphorically 'smell the roses', and experience the world as it is. It looked like a complete break from the rush and chaos of an office, and is definitely something I feel many of us miss out on – time set aside just to relax.

I sat down close to them and looked around; magnificent buildings all around me, families ushering their little children away from the forbidden to walk on areas, the feel of the grass on my legs as I lay down, the smell of street food frying up on a nearby stand, and the complete feeling of relaxation as my mind cleared of absolutely everything else and made itself fully present. My surroundings were the only thing at all in my consciousness.

Action: At the risk of sounding like a new-age hippie or yoga teacher (which my hamstring flexibility would not allow!) I fully recommend that, in your busy life today, you take a second to just 'be.' Be mindful of what is around you, instead of keeping your mind full. This could be through listening to music, going for a walk, meditating, drawing a picture, listening to the sounds of nature, or anything else you can think of, but take a few moments today and each day to just be still. Life moves fast, often too fast, as we try to control every area of our existence. We often do not give ourselves enough time to be still, to allow insights to come into our mind, and to simply be present and mindful. Today, give yourself that opportunity.

Lesson #23

Life on your own terms

In my 24 years so far I've been fortunate enough to visit almost 60 countries; however, more than a third of those were destinations I fleetingly visited while working on a cruise ship. Those short trips, often with just a few days ashore, didn't allow enough time to really engage with the city or culture and see what it was all about. Of course, that has its pros and cons – and really just means I need to go back and revisit some of those places properly!

It's pretty common for time-constrained travellers to check out TripAdvisor when planning a trip. This is great to help you decide on a plan, and what to see during your stay. In fact, during my first few weeks in Shanghai and the surrounding cities, I did exactly that. Some of the advice was great, some of it less so.

I'm sure many people who follow me on social networks are aware from my many photos of food that local cuisine is a very important part of my enjoyment while travelling. Therefore, in my initial weeks, I was really pleased to hear about a TripAdvisor-backed dumpling restaurant close to Yu Garden, a beautiful but very touristy area of the city. Of course I had to try it out and, as one of my first experiences of eating dumplings here, I thought there could be no better place. A few mouthfuls and much disappointment later, I have to confess they were pretty average dumplings, and the large queue outside the shop was most likely full of people who'd read the same reviews I had.

Fast forward a few weeks to today: I was hungry and walking down a street near People's Park metro station, and decided to eat in whichever place had the biggest queue. There was no doubt about which it was, so I joined the line of hungry people. What followed was an interesting demonstration of how crab and pork dumplings are put together, and a taste experience on a completely different level to the previous dumplings. The crab tasted so fresh, the ginger accompanying the dishes so pungent, while the mix of juices and the thin, wrappers encasing the dumplings were just right. When friends and family come to town, this is where I will be taking them. It's hard to go wrong when such a large number of locals are waiting outside!

As fun and potentially simple as it may be to follow a guide, I think there is much more merit in going out there, forging your own path and seeing what comes up as a result of that. The world is too big to try and follow someone else's ideas and, if you do, you may miss out on the best of the best crab shēngjiānbāo.

Action: Have a look at your life and what you've achieved in the last five years. Have you flawlessly followed a traditional route to get to where you are? Perhaps some freak encounters led to unexpected developments and opportunities. If this is the case, as it seems to be for many people, try to let go of some of the desire to plan each and every aspect of your life. Try not to follow what the TripAdvisors of the world may want you to believe, and instead decide to find your own way. Even if you don't find the best dumplings, I'm sure your adventure into the unknown will make the story more fun to recall.

Lesson #24

Taking advantage of what is around you

Since arriving in Shanghai I've been able to watch and take part in so many interesting activities. When I speak to people who've been here a lot longer than me, they are often surprised by how much I've managed to cram in.

As it happens, I work five and a half or six days a week, largely because I love my job, but also manage to find time for a lot of extra stuff too. This often surprises people who assume I work one day a week and have the rest free as travel time!

One of the main benefits of my current location is that Shanghai is one of the world's major cities and, as a result, many large-scale events happen to pass by. The fact the metro and transport system is so huge and accessible really helps too, but if you keep your eyes open you will find there is always a lot going on.

In the last few weeks there has been the Shanghai F1 and international beach volleyball competitions, as well as 'X-games' extreme sports events, and tonight was the 'Shanghai Diamond League', where many of the best athletes in the world come to compete in a one-night event.

I was coaching today until 6pm but decided that, having been offered tickets, I would see which friends were interested and then make my way to the local metro for the 30-minute journey to the stadium. I'd never been to the area, so my friends and I had a brief exploration and picked up a quick meal before heading inside the stadium.

I don't think I had ever seen a live steeplechase race before, but the absurdity of it quickly made it a favourite. The water the athletes jumped into was a lot deeper than I'd imagined, and watching the cameramen get soaked on the first lap, as they misjudged how close they could get without getting splashed, was especially amusing.

All around the stadium, the discus, jumping events, hurdles, and 100 metre sprints were taking place. Between the world-class athletics and a standard selection of silly pictures, videos and jokes with friends, it went down as another great evening in Shanghai. I caught the last train home, crashed on my bed, and didn't wake up till 4am, by which time I'd missed several planned Skype calls! For a pretty low key, simple to organise, and virtually free evening, it was well worth it.

I don't often believe it when people say they don't have enough time or money to do much other than work and sleep. I've had some of my funniest Shanghai memories joining in a free street Tai Chi class, and meeting up with friends to watch a free open mic comedy show. All it takes is a willingness to explore, a passion for adventure, and a desire to live as interesting a life as possible.

Action: Life is for living...go and make some memories! Note down two activities you could do on your next day off, or perhaps one evening after work. Challenge yourself to try out a few of these activities in the upcoming week. The more you explore and see what is around, the more it seems that there is to do. How does having a rich and full life of new and varied experiences sound?

CHINESE REALISATION OF THE DAY

Making people laugh doesn't require much language skill. Despite my Chinese having improved quite a bit recently, I had this lady in stitches after telling her (in very basic Chinese) that her Chinese speaking is very good, with as straight a face as I could manage.

CHINESE REALISATION OF THE DAY

If you hit your ankle with your scooter right on an existing scab, it hurts. If you hit almost the same spot just 30 minutes later, you will be left hobbling and really irritated. If, after dinner, you hit the same spot as you turn a corner, you may or may not let out a loud enough noise that the Chinese man next to you lets out a little yelp and then drops his small bag of groceries... Fortunately, the hilarity of his reaction numbed the pain maybe 5% and I made it home with no more scrapes!

CHINESE REALISATION OF THE DAY

If you go to the museum and want to try out a few of the sport exhibits in China, be careful as some of them may be designed for kids. You may have an inflated feeling of self-worth as you win a £5 bet with a Chinese man that you can lift the heaviest 1RM deadlift weight that all of the locals are struggling with. This feeling will continue as you get loud cheers from impressed locals as your speed is highest on the football penalty kick machine, but you will be promptly brought back down to earth as the penalty kick you smash at the brick wall bounces back, hits a young, spectacled girl in the face, and makes her cry...

CHINESE REALISATION OF THE DAY

Just because your taxi driver is making VERY realistic snoring noises as he is driving, does not mean you need to be alarmed. If this situation does arise and you give him a little tap, you will really confuse the poor guy and even make him slightly angry. Don't worry though; all can be rectified by using your limited Chinese to tell him the building you just passed is very big... Confused looks and sounds all round!

CHINESE REALISATION OF THE DAY

Chinese hairdressers can be ridiculous places. I go in, ask for a number two and he starts. Two minutes later, I'm done. Simples. I then exclaim how easy that was and he must feel I'm upset, as he then spends the next ten minutes cutting imaginary bits of hair off before randomly getting stuck in to my facial hair before I could say no. The cutthroat razor with no cream wasn't the most comfortable, and left me looking like a prepubescent boy, but all was made up for when I got a free hair wash and he insisted on giving me my first blow dry of my life...on my almost bald head!

CHINESE REALISATION OF THE DAY

If you want to see your assistant get REALLY embarrassed, be in a car with him when he drives past a bus stop after heavy rain and absolutely drenches the people waiting. The funniest part of the situation was that he didn't realise, and then was mortified when I explained why I was laughing so hard!

Lesson #25

Put the phone down

In this increasingly mobile world, with more and more emphasis on 'social interaction', it is becoming increasingly normal to watch people spend long periods in the presence of others without actually spending any time in the presence of others. Smartphones have become the source of much distraction and, worse still, a subsequent disengagement from the real world in front of them.

As much as I love social media and the connection it gives me to friends, family and followers worldwide, this is not all good. As an experiment, I recently decided not to use my phone during the 30-minute journey I took into town to meet a friend for dinner. Maybe it was a coincidence, but the moments I experienced seemed different during this trip...

- I was used as a human resting post for two apparently extremely tired Chinese men.

My thrilling conversation does it again!

- As I got up and gestured to an older Chinese man that my seat was for him, he gave me the biggest, toothiest grin and looked incredibly pleased.

- A middle-aged man, who had seemingly never seen a foreign person before, decided to stare particularly hard at me for what seemed like forever. As I looked up and caught him staring at me, not for the first time, I saw that he also had his phone in his hand and was preparing to take a picture. I quickly pulled a face for the camera, before pulling out my iPad, striking a photographer's pose, and taking a picture of him too. He clearly found the absurdity of the situation as amusing as me, and we both laughed before looking away, and moving on with life, with the addition of another ridiculous photo each...

- I had a light-hearted staring contest with the toddler sitting on the lap of the woman next to me. This quickly escalated, with the baby trying to grab my hand, squirm away from Mum and come to stand on my lap. Later on, this same baby leaned forwards and tried to slap me, all the while with a cute, innocent little baby smile on its face. While all this was going on, I was chatting with the child's mother in broken Chinese, so having to avoid being slapped in the face at the same time was quite amusing and, as I left the train, the smiles and wave from both mother and baby made for a brilliant moment. The mother even called out 'goodbye, nice to meet you' in English.

On a recent trip to Hong Kong, I set myself a reduced internet experiment and I'm able to confirm that I survived. Emails that were sent may not have received replies until I batched them with a few others later, but this slight delay didn't cause me any problems. Comments on articles I had written, friend requests and likes on pictures may not have been noted straightaway, but life still went on. In fact, it was an important reminder that, although we do have so much instant communication these days, it's easy to get bogged down in the assumption that everything requires an instant response. That false sense of urgency can leave us feeling like we're always chasing our tails, being reactive instead of proactive. As a result, I spent far more of my time in the present, on the really valuable things.

Wherever you are in the world, there are so many situations just waiting to play out each day. If you think back to how you met a friend, so many separate coincidences probably had to occur to enable that first meeting to happen. Perhaps having your head down, buried in your phone, may mean you miss out on potentially life-changing encounters. I don't think it is worth the risk.

Action: The next time you're out for a meal, with friends, or on public transport, make a conscious decision to avoid your phone. Experience the world around, instead of letting it flash by unrecognised while your attention is solely on the screen in front of you. The moments that occur are often far more thrilling than receiving a retweet, Instagram like, or Facebook poke. Turn off instant email notifications and instead commit to only checking emails at certain times during the day, perhaps at intervals of a few hours. Hardly anything is so important that it has to be replied to straightaway and, if it is, it will more likely be rectified by an instant phone call than a few lines of text. Find out which activities in your life are constantly derailing you from productivity, and ask yourself honestly if it needs to be that way. When you realise it doesn't, try toning those areas down and enjoy the world around with new eyes.

Mobile phone addiction has certainly hit Shanghai across all age groups

Lesson #26

Plan incessantly, get it wrong and carry on, or go with the flow?

As I woke up, I did my daily check of 'Timehop' – the app that tells me what I posted on various social media sites on this day in previous years. It's been very interesting for me in the past few months to look back and remember what I've been up to. Coupled with a conversation today with a new friend, I reflected on a few things:

- In the past five years I've crammed in a lot of excitement: I've enjoyed many new experiences; travelled a lot; eaten great food; seen great sights; spent time with fantastic people; taken part in some crazy activities; developed a lot as a person; and so much more. I would not change much of what I've done and how it has all panned out.

- If I'd had to predict five years ago what I could accomplish and how my career would develop, I would not even have come close to predicting what has really unfolded. Even as an eternal optimist – and at times unrealistic dreamer – I would never have imagined it to be this good.

- Who knows where I will be in five more years.

Last year, another friend told me that the only right path for me is my path, and if I'm following directly in somebody else's footprints then it's not mine. A simple but profound comment, highlighting that if I ever try to follow someone else's route then I won't be being true to myself, and will likely miss out on opportunities along the way. That's not to say I should live life with no plans, be completely carefree, and assume it will all come together at some point, but it is fine to keep progressing, knowing you can't predict the future. Each bit of progress in one area may lead to an opportunity in another and, before you know it, an outcome that's nowhere near what you might have imagined in your wildest dreams. In fact, a lot of the crazy opportunities I've been fortunate enough to have so far happened just that way.

Going to University was part of a bigger plan for me. I knew the experiences I had, the people I met, and the qualifications I came away with would help me as I progressed in my career. However, in retrospect, it was completely different areas of my university life that actually enabled me to reach my current position. I just could not possibly have predicted how many interlinking pieces would be woven together, resulting in my current place in life. That's fun and exciting, but also potentially devastating if you like trying to control every part of your life and future.

Action: Try to remember, picture or discuss where you were on this date at a moment in the past. Now compare that to where you are now. Not only can this be an extremely positive way to see just how much you've developed and moved on; it can also help you powerfully prove to yourself how little you would have been able to predict, but how good the outcome has been anyway.

Lesson #27

Surround yourself with smart people and it might even rub off!

If you look around at any of the best companies or business teams in the world you will quickly see that they are much stronger together than their individual parts. Similarly, no successful sports team can function on just one superstar; instead, the team must work coherently to achieve the best results.

Robleato Children's Home, San Jose, Costa Rica

In the time I've spent travelling around the world, and throughout the rest my life, I've been lucky to spend time with lots of different people, from all walks of life, who have no doubt helped shape me into who I am today: company CEOs, who come to me for golf lessons; the children I worked with in a Costa Rican orphanage; the many Shanghai taxi drivers I try to chat with; and everybody else in between. I'm sure I've learnt something about myself or the world in each of these interactions, and I've tried to take on the best bits, the knowledge, wisdom, humility, and many other characteristics I admire, from the people I've met.

This evening I was called wise. Now, that may not seem particularly significant, or even worth noting down, but to me it was.

I've always been comfortable around people and used to assume that simply researching a lot and becoming proficient in many areas of golf technique would enable me to become a better coach. That would have worked as a route to becoming a moderate golf coach, but that wasn't enough; I wanted to be the best I possibly could be. This ambition lead me to spend a lot of time travelling the world, hanging out with many of the smartest minds I could – who I'm proud that I can now call friends – and, as a result, I have developed massively.

I've realised that coaching is much more about the person, and that the sport-specific skills are often a minuscule part of the job. I've learnt more about individual differences and getting the most out of each performer, and I've discovered the satisfaction of helping people reach their own, wildly individual goals. I've been able to discover all of this, have conversations that have broadened my horizons, and glean wisdom from a whole host of people. I have also been constantly astounded at how giving people are with their time, energy, and even money, when they are helping out others who have a passion. To say that I've been fortunate would be an understatement, and this is something I now try to play forward as people come to me for advice.

Making mistakes and learning from them is a great way to develop, however you can save yourself a lot of time in the future if you invest time, and maybe even money, now on learning, observing, and questioning what those before you have done.

As an added bonus, this will often lead to ridiculously good networking opportunities, which might otherwise have been unreachable. So much good has happened through deciding what I wanted to achieve and, at the same time, deciding on the best way to go about meeting people who could help. You never know just what opportunities can present themselves when you branch out and mix with lots of different people, instead of settling with one small group.

Action: In an area of your life that you're interested in developing, I challenge you to write a list of six people who you believe could help you to better yourself. Two of these should be people who you feel are unlikely to respond and are far too busy to help you out; two should be people who you believe could potentially respond and allow you to share some time with them; and, finally, two should be people who you're 100% sure will be welcoming, yet who you could still find value in spending time with. Send a handwritten letter, make a phone call, or ask for a recommendation from a mutual friend, and make contact. The rest of the action is up to you, but the challenge is to initiate that first contact within 24 hours. Your time starts...now!

Lights. Camera. Action! On the set for my first live TV show talking about Golf in China

Lesson #28

Madness

So much madness occurs every day in this country that to write it all down wouldn't leave me time to do anything else. Just this week, a friend and I had a jokey 20-minute argument with a train attendant, who wasn't allowing her to take her helium-filled balloon onto the metro. As we were in no rush, we played along, spoke to multiple metro workers, pretended to be upset, attempted to board the train, and were advised to just pop the balloon and take it on board that way. After much calamity, confusion, and being told there was no chance, we were shadily given a big black plastic bag to put the balloon in, and allowed to travel.

I've also been to IKEA this week and, other than stocking up on meatballs and Dime bars, a small group of us spent a few hours having a great laugh: sitting in the beds, cracking jokes, making new friends, chatting about life, playing games of hide and seek, and confusing the staff. I should also point out that just last year China supposedly passed a law stating it was not illegal to kick out families who came for day trips to IKEA and were caught sleeping on the beds, which is apparently quite common. The fact that making ourselves comfortable in the beds hardly raised a glance from staff makes this sound pretty plausible.

Today I visited Thames Town, a pretty town designed in an English style, with cobbled streets; red phone boxes; guards in red; brick buildings; a replica of Christ Church, Bristol; and statues, street names, restaurants, shops and features that do all feel quite English – along with customary rain too. Strangely though, the town was almost completely deserted; every restaurant, bar, library and shop only appeared to be housing their own staff. It really felt like you were on a film set – especially as the only non-working occupants were various Chinese couples taking part in photo shoots, and being transported around with big cameras in golf buggies! According to friends, this is how it was five years ago, and I imagine it's been losing money all this time.

Initially I would have witnessed these goings-on and exclaimed at the madness of China, now I look deeper. A little research showed that the static of a helium balloon once caused a large electrical fire, which shut down a tube network in America for a full day. Chinese families go on day trips to IKEA for the air conditioning, cheap food, and free kids' play areas. Lastly, Thames town was built as a holiday retreat and, despite houses initially being snapped up very fast, they were largely bought as second homes for wealthy families; the town therefore stays eerily deserted for many weeks of the year.

Action: Think of a situation that confuses you at present. Maybe you cannot comprehend how a co-worker can be so grumpy or disagreeable, or why Chinese people always push you further onto the metro when you're trying to exit. In each case, try to see the logic and other person's point of view, or what may have happened previously to reach this point. Having a bit of compassion in this way will help your own sanity, as well as making you better able to understand those all around you.

Note: I'm sure what I just said doesn't apply to everything in China; some things really are just crazy!

CHINESE REALISATION OF THE DAY

Twenty minutes of jokily dancing with slightly older ladies in the park will be more tiring than you imagine and also involve lots of smiles, ridiculously catchy Chinese songs, surprised faces, and being invited back for the next day!

When in China, do as the locals do!

CHINESE REALISATION OF THE DAY

Some Chinese restaurants will apparently chop your beef up for you, in front of you, at the table. Not entirely sure if it was a service thing, lack of trust in my knife skills, or not thinking I could cope with just chopsticks, but it provided another interesting China moment – especially as this process took quite a while!

CHINESE REALISATION OF THE DAY

Apparently this city has more than one black Mercedes people carrier…I come out of my apartment block to meet the company driver to take me to the course. I spot a car close by where he normally comes. I open the door, say hey and go to take a seat. Unfortunately, not the right car and the look from the confused guy was beyond priceless.

CHINESE REALISATION OF THE DAY

If you are going to play a game of 'challenges' in IKEA, be careful: not ALL Chinese people are as open to having pictures of them taken as they are to get snap happy, without asking, right in your face, during any situation! One of the seemingly simple challenges I was set, of getting a selfie with a worker, resulted in me being turned down by the first lady I asked and then very angry stares from the second, who wanted the photo deleted, followed by more scowls and severe hostility. On the plus side, I did complete the challenge; unfortunately, the situation got a little bit worse when the angry lady in question went and explained what had happened to the very same lady who had turned me down first. I'm still weighing up whether passing the challenge and continuing a hilarious few hours in IKEA was worth feeling like I was about to be murdered by two middle-aged Chinese ladies every time I turned round a corner in the store…

CHINESE REALISATION OF THE DAY

I will never understand what goes through the mind of some Chinese people. Today, just outside South Shaanxi metro station, I saw a woman who must have been almost 70 going for a run. Pretty impressive, I'd think, and the fact she was in full Nike workout gear (including headband!) was equally so and kind of adorable. With that in mind, what on earth went on in her mind to think that wearing three inch heels for this evening activity was wise, I'll never know!

Lesson #29

Making an effort

Almost every single day, as I return to my apartment block after work, there is a guy sitting on his scooter at the entrance, waiting to offer his services as a driver. He seems like a nice guy, we always have a very basic conversation, and I let him know if I'll be in need of a ride that day. Given the convenience of his location, compared to trying to hail a cab on the road, and the fact he charges me less than the minimum charge of the real taxis to get to the metro, I quite often ride with him.

I wonder how many people rely on him for transport, as I always seem to be the only one, and he often appears to be there from at least 6-11PM. If his workload is as quiet as I think, that's a pretty lowly hourly rate for sure. On occasion I've given him more money than the fare, and his face has erupted into a smile as he thanked me, but that's for another story. Today what he showed was a perfect example of customer service, and how to ensure I always spend my money with him.

As I work in what I would term the entertainment and service industry, I know it's important that everyone who spends time and money with me feels that they enjoy our sessions, as well as improving their golf. It's often some of the smallest differences that lead to very satisfied golfers, by ensuring the finer details and expectations of each lesson are met. Something that may be relatively cheap and simple to implement can make a huge difference to how happy a client is.

Today, as I walked into my apartment block, I told the driver I would be back in an hour, as I needed to get ready and have food before heading to town to meet friends. As I later emerged, it was raining, dark, no taxis were in sight, and more importantly, neither was he. A bit annoyed that he wasn't there, as I'd come out at exactly the time we'd agreed, I crossed the road, ready to head towards the metro station and attempt to find a cab on the way. Not long after I had crossed the road, I heard the beeping of a horn and realised it was him, coming from the opposite direction. It later transpired that he had driven up and down the road, attempting to find me, and must have missed me at first. He pulled over, put the umbrella on the back of his scooter up, and handed me a towel to dry myself with. Going out of his way to try to amend his mistake, and ensure I got the ride as intended, really impressed me and fell right in line with one of my favourite quotes:

"Do not over-promise and under-deliver, instead under-promise and over-deliver."

Early on in my coaching career, while I was working in Miami I was given some incredibly useful advice: Approach each and every lesson you give as if it's being paid for with the last few pennies of that person's money. The fact that it's the last lesson of a long day, or that it's not for a big-time CEO or high level golfer, is no excuse to give anything other than your absolute best. Each and every person is equally deserving of your time and attention – it's an important lesson as a coach, but also as a human being, in going that extra mile to help those around.

Action: Exceeding someone's expectations does not take lavish gifts. A simple phone call to a friend, a card or flowers sent home on a day other than Mother's Day to say how grateful you are; or a cold glass of water and refreshing towel when a golfer arrives on a warm day – is often enough to dramatically exceed expectations. Your challenge: in three ways today, go out of your way to exceed someone else's expectations. Maybe it will be noticed, maybe it won't, but I can assure you that the results will show in the long run. In this particular case, the scooter driver retained his best customer. Today, also, try to give some time, or something of value, to someone who normally wouldn't receive much of your time or attention. Maybe it's offering a drink to the Big Issue seller, or perhaps just a smile to the lollipop lady helping kids cross the road. Perhaps it's leaving a decent tip for your waiter at the restaurant, or making the time to speak to your next-door neighbour. Whatever it is, remember that each and every person on this planet is as valuable as any other and deserves to smile, just as we all do.

Service with a smile...and a rain hood!

Lesson #30

Ice, ice baby

Living in China during the football World Cup is a challenge. The number of 4am games I've stayed up for is frightening; I'm lucky I don't require masses of sleep and can still function the next day! Last night, after a night out, we decided to watch the Costa Rica game – as it's one of my favourite nations in the whole world. My love affair started when I spent two consecutive summers volunteering in an orphanage, falling in love with the people and culture, and trying to improve life for as many people as I could. The people's warmth and passion, alongside positivity in adversity, instantly made me a fan. One thing I wasn't a fan of though was the ice-cold showers...

I definitely had fewer showers than anyone doing manual labour in sweltering heat should; retrospectively, I'm sorry to those who were around me – I just could not deal with the cold! I remember splashing water onto myself, or gradually edging in, but to no avail; it was a challenge that I failed. Being a stubborn guy, I'm sure you can imagine that this failure didn't leave my head and, in the last few weeks, taking ice cold showers (partly for the health benefits, yet mainly due to not liking to feel like I've been beaten) has been one of my weekly challenges. I started with an increased desire to succeed as I inched in, splashed water on myself, and even put my waterproof headphones on, blaring my favourite songs to try and help distract myself. Nope. Mere seconds later I was out, and this continued until I realised the same input would keep giving me the same output!

The next day I turned the shower to ice-cold, put my music on and put my whole body straightaway under the water. The initial shock was compounded by an immense feeling of satisfaction and, before I knew it, I had adapted. I carried on as normal and almost forgot it was ice-cold water. It started to feel so normal that I went to make the water even colder. I stepped out of the spray, and only when I went back in did I realise how cold it really was. By not overthinking the situation, and instead just plunging in, I had managed to conquer my fear without much effort at all. By challenging myself with something small like this, I was developing my mind. Building this kind of mental strength is like building muscle; the more exercise you give it, the stronger it becomes. The stronger we are, the more we can take on challenges, deal with ups and downs, and keep our emotions under control, so we can make better choices in other situations. Sounds like it's worth developing to me!

Action: Think of the most difficult task in your day – the one that would be easy to put off. Write it down and get it done first. That workout you could easily skip? Get it done before other things take priority. Getting your tax form completed before it becomes a hassle and you face late fees... All these situations can be made better if the right action is taken and you persevere with the 'ice-cold shower' tasks first. Talking yourself out of them, justifying why they're not possible, and putting these things off never helps. I've managed to conquer the fear, make ice showers feel almost pleasant, and I'm still alive to tell the tale. If this is possible for me, what fears can you overcome?

Lesson #31

Things taken for granted

The last few days have certainly been a bit of a challenge over here in Asia. My electricity has largely been off, which has left me unable to see much, stay warm, charge anything, and has therefore limited my communication methods. Additionally, my cooker has been playing up and a problem with my mobile phone contract means I've also been inexplicably left without a phone service or internet, making it impossible to contact my landlord about fixing the other problems in the apartment. Fortunately I've been out of the apartment quite a bit, spending time with various new friends, who've kept me in decent spirits and prevented me from turning into an unwashed, hungry, unshaven, communication-withdrawn mess!

It took the loss of things that I consider such basic necessities to really remember just how fortunate I am. Despite all of the hassle, less than 72 hours after the initial problems, everything is back as it should be. My time without these commonly taken for granted utilities are nothing compared to a lifetime of going without for many in this world.

"It's not happy people who are thankful. It's thankful people who are happy."

This quote reminds me of quite possibly the happiest, most contented person I ever met, in Grenada, during the time I spent teaching golf on a cruise ship. His simple life consisted of morning swims with his family before chauffeuring people around his beloved island, giving guided tours, and then relaxing over a BBQ dinner with family on the beach, and maybe a run along the shore before bed. Such a simple life but you could sense, in everything he did, how grateful he was. His endless storytelling and the thankfulness he expressed for his island, family, and lifestyle are, I am sure, what helped make him the warm, smiling soul that he was.

If somebody had asked me, before I left, to write a list of things from England that I imagined I'd miss, I'm not sure what I would have put. Of course, friends and family would've been there and, unsurprisingly, that is still true. However, I had been given a lot of out-dated advice about day-to-day life – for example, that credit cards are not readily useable. Despite it being a largely cash-based society, things like that haven't even remotely been an issue. I'd heard that watching Western TV shows would be tough without using a VPN (Virtual Private Network) to mask my location online. This is true, but not an issue thanks to the million and one DVD shops all around. I likely would have mentioned a few of my favourite food items, but my willingness to try new things meant that, although I knew there would be challenges, I accepted that life halfway across the world would be different and was fine with that. What I've realised though, is how many things you take for granted, and those are the things I've really missed.

In my time here, due to pollution, I have seen blue skies just a handful of times, and several of those were during a couple of consecutive days in Beijing, right at the beginning – almost as if China was trying to ease me in gently. Seeing the outline of the sun, but it being obscured by clouds of pollution is a real nuisance and, as soon as the blue sky does appear for a day, you miss it even more when it goes. I will certainly be more grateful for clean air when I visit home, or wherever else my future may take me. You wouldn't believe how much joy it brought me to be able to visit a park last week, play football barefoot, and enjoy the crisp green grass, with the blue of the sky above, on a rare clear day.

Of course, I knew the language would be an issue when I moved, but it had never occurred to me before to be grateful that I lived in a country where communicating with the majority of those around me was so simple. I am persevering with my Chinese, but the moment when a fluent English-speaker comes by and understands your sarcasm, bad one-liner jokes and crazy anecdotes, and can therefore see the complete version of you as a person, is still so gratifying.

Action: Today, note down three things that you are thankful for; maybe things you generally take for granted but that are actually huge blessings. Perhaps it is clean water, a country at peace, the gift of being able to live without fear of your surroundings, the ability to witness the wonder of the world with all of your senses, being able to comfortably live through all of the seasons, or that you have had an education that can allow you to prosper. It is often easy to think of three special events that have happened during the day but try to make one of the three something 'ordinary' that you take for granted. After today, each evening try to note down one more thing and, before too long, you will have a big long list of things that you are blessed to have, which will put you well on the way to realising the wealth of opportunities and blessings you have in your life. From personal experience, I really believe this will help you to live a happier life.

View of The Bund, Shanghai

Lesson #32

Thinking you're better

It is always interesting looking at the external lives of fellow expats in a crazy place like Shanghai. You have those who appear to have settled in well and integrated into the madness. Like me, I'm sure they have frequent dinners with friends where they share their crazy, strange and frustrating experiences, but overall they laugh off concerns and stay positive. At the other end, you get the people for whom the weather is always too hot or cold, and the pollution too terrible; who are unable to find home comforts, and, when you combine all that with communication issues and local habits like spitting on the street, they really don't seem all that enamoured.

Watching interactions between foreigners and locals is also interesting. Sadly, I've seen too many situations where local workers are treated poorly, or as lesser beings, by Westerners and this saddens me. The incongruence between how that Westerner acts here, compared to how they must function to be accepted back in their own country, is vast and frustrates me. I've seen people throw their cash in the general direction of waitresses, with no eye contact, and force them to pick up the money as it rolls on the floor, with no apology – and many other sad examples besides. At the end of the day, they and I are visitors in this country; we shouldn't expect it to be just like our own, but should treat those here with respect.

The full-time driver of one of the extremely wealthy clients at the academy seems to have a great situation. At every meal I've shared with this client and his friends, the driver has always been present. He is part of the group, and treated with respect by all – and, as a result, gives his best effort back to make sure he meets the needs of his boss.

My assistant recently went out of his way to help me on his day off, when a few unavoidable circumstances meant I'd been left on my own. It was a challenging day as I was busy with lessons, but he came and helped me get the place in order so I could get on with teaching. In return, I jokingly served all the duties that he usually performs for me, getting the golf balls and a glass of water ready before giving him some help with his game, while he stayed and practised. I thanked him genuinely and also bought him a little gift, because he'd gone out of his way to help me out and thoroughly deserved it.

In both these situations, the end result was better output from the worker involved, as they felt more valued – a win-win situation!

In a similar vein, I always smile and wave at the cleaner who sweeps leaves every morning around my apartment block. I'd like to think her toothy grin back at me is genuine and she appreciates the contact, but I also feel like I win, as I share a little bit of love in a very simple way each morning.

Action: Go out of your way today to make somebody else feel valued for what they do for you or others. Often their actions or work may be taken for granted or overlooked but, as I constantly see, giving people the recognition they deserve can be hugely motivating and empowering. Instead of only reaching out and speaking up when there's an issue, try to genuinely show satisfaction when things are done well, and become known for sharing joy and gratitude, not consistently complaining.

CHINESE REALISATION OF THE DAY

What do Chinese people do with all of the pictures and videos they take? I'm hardly immune to taking a few pictures; I take many to try and remember a lot of the daily madness. I also get that my face doesn't fit in with most of the other 25,000,000+ people in this city and so I expect some of the pictures that are taken of me. I really would LOVE to know, however, what the same lady does with the four videos of me exercising at the gym yesterday. After looking questioningly at what I was doing and chatting to a trainer, she then filmed all four sets that I did...puzzling!

CHINESE REALISATION OF THE DAY

If I ever move back to England, I'll be in trouble. I crack a lot of smiles and silly faces at the locals here and in return receive lots of smiles. When eye contact is made not once, not twice, but three times as an inquisitive local checks me out, I'm not sure holding this eye contact and then pulling a face, which eventually leads to the local letting out a huge grin, would go down so well back home...

CHINESE REALISATION OF THE DAY

Chinese taxi drivers never fail to take me by surprise. I am having a lovely 20 minute chat in Chinese with the taxi man this morning. We talk about golf, Tiger Woods, the weather (of course, I am English!), which English accent is easiest to understand and much more. He seems a great guy and says how much he likes foreigners as he learnt some English from them. He then tells me about how I should get a Shanghai girlfriend and I say yes, maybe it would be useful for speaking the language... ...he looks at me and laughs and says "no, I mean for the sucky sucky."

CHINESE REALISATION OF THE DAY

At 7am, old Chinese ladies might be the best personal trainers you'll ever have. I'm in the gym, getting the customary glances and stares. I put out a box for some plyometric jumps and do the first set. Three Chinese ladies on exercise bikes look over the whole time and, in between my sets of jumps, shout out encouragingly...'one more.' I agree and think the box could go higher, so I make the change. They look over during the next set, clapping each and every jump I make. I then think I could make the box even a little bit higher, so I increase the height, to huge applause and gasps from them, who have by now completely stopped their own training and are just clapping away, having the time of their lives...never a dull moment!

CHINESE REALISATION OF THE DAY

Workout attire is different here. Today I saw a guy stretching in a suit in the gym and then this evening, as I walk back into my apartment block at around 6pm, running towards me is a guy in a suit, tie and dress shoes. No big deal, I think... likely late for a meeting. It is a little bit more confusing as, after I carry on, he suddenly appears again, having done a mini lap. Naive me thinks perhaps he's just forgotten something for said meeting... The third time I see him, I am almost back at my block. He is doubled over, panting, and sipping from a workout bottle. As I walk past and turn around in confusion, I see him again... this time, dropped down and cranking out a few push-ups!

Lesson #33

Making time

Ten Thousand Buddhas Monastery, Hong Kong – just trying to fit in...

As someone who very rarely finds himself ill, these last two days have been a real struggle. After having dinner out the other night, I got home and went to bed, only to wake up to the sensation that somebody was stamping on my head while, simultaneously, someone else was inside my head, trying to escape with a pick axe! This pain whenever I moved or breathed lasted for two whole days and, despite trying to persevere and continue coaching for five hours on the first day, I spent from 5pm on Sunday night until 3pm on Monday in bed, only getting up as I had packing to do and a flight to catch.

In typical positive fashion, I was able to conclude a few things.

Firstly, that I am very fortunate this is such a rare occurrence, as many people have these kinds of aches and pains far more frequently. It would be very easy to get down and wonder why I got this mystery illness, but I think more realistically I should be looking at it the other way around, and marvelling at how my body functions pretty wonderfully 99% of the time.

Secondly, for maybe the first time in my life, I had to cancel work, as on the second day I simply couldn't face moving – let alone being energetic and motivational in the way my golfers are used to me being. I therefore had an enforced stay in bed and, during that time, managed to watch two films I'd been meaning to see for a long time, read through some interesting looking articles that I'd been saving until I had time, and also made a few Skype calls to friends who I happened to spot online. All of these would generally have been things I'd love to do if I had time, but in this situation the time was made for me.

While I wouldn't advise skipping work to catch up on personal things, it was a great reminder to me to consider how I spend my other hours, and what else I would have been doing outside of work on that day that would have limited my time for all those activities.

Action: I hate the idea of guilt tripping somebody into a decision, but I am all for honest evaluations, which can often allow people to independently reach the same conclusion and make the same changes. My challenge to you today is, for the next 72 hours, write down what your time is being filled with. Of course, sleeping, working, preparing and eating food, and other regular tasks always need doing, but you may be surprised by how much other 'stuff' fills your day. How much improvement would you see overall if you replaced that 'stuff' with something more meaningful, valuable and resourceful that you've perhaps been putting off 'until you have time'?

Lesson #34

The joy of discovering and exploring

From speaking to many others, and spending so much time travelling myself, I can sympathise with the view that you can initially love a place, acting like a tourist, with wide-eyed anticipation while everything is new, sparkly and fresh, but then mundaneness hits and suddenly everything seems too familiar and less appealing. I'm sure for many this is perfectly normal, but in a city that boasts a larger population than Sweden, New Zealand and the entire United Arab Emirates combined, I'm sure there's more than enough to see and do to fill up many years – and by that point, more will have been built anyway!

In the last few weeks, a couple of friends and I have noted down activities we'd love to try but have never got round to, or just haven't done for a while. So far I've managed quite a few from the list; just this week, I've crammed in Salsa, Bachata and Tango dancing, Tai Chi, laser quest, shooting, Chinese lessons, a yoga class, and trying out a new gym, all in addition to my normal socialising, dinners, living, working, and sleeping.

With all these new skills, I've really valued the learning experience, as well as the fantastic new friends I've gained. Being a student again, learning completely new skills, has not only been immensely satisfying but has also given me a new, deeper empathy for my beginner golfers. Of course, Salsa is also very popular with the ladies here, so it's been great in that department too!

There hasn't been a single one of these sessions I haven't enjoyed, although I don't think I'll stick at some of them beyond the free trial session. As much fun as it was walking around in circles, making Chinese women blush as they had to place their hands on my chest during tango, it didn't really seem like something I wanted to spend a lot of time on.

Out of all these activities, Bachata dancing is the one I'm giving most attention to. A few weeks in, I love the music, the feeling of being completely helpless and a total beginner, the ability to see improvement, the number of new and interesting people, the friendly vibe of the scene, and the fact that each and every person seems ecstatic to be there, and bursting with life as they dance, even when making 'mistakes' and treading on other people's toes (OK…maybe that's just me!)

As someone who spends my career putting smiles on the faces of often extremely wealthy people, who would love nothing more than to play better golf, I understand the drive to improve. The thrill of working with a new golfer, who starts to improve and go beyond their own expectations, is amazing. Watching someone discover what they could be capable of, and gaining confidence as a result, is something that goes much deeper than just the acquiring of a better golf swing.

Personally, I've spent a lot of my life improving myself, sacrificing endless hours to become a better athlete, coach, person, and developing skills in a range of different areas. However, I had forgotten just how addictive learning a new skill can be. Since joining this Bachata class, I have discovered a completely new world, where people dance to this type of music every single night of the week; I've rediscovered the thrill of experiencing something new, as you browse YouTube videos, search out classes, and download new music, all in an effort to improve; and I've seen myself go from vastly incompetent to moderately incompetent – almost always with a smile on my face.

Learning some Tai Chi on the sly in a park

Action: You know that list of things you'd really like to do? Make no excuses and take action today to get one of those going. Pick up the phone, research a class, and go for it. You never know where the journey will take you; perhaps you will try a class and decide it isn't for you, but maybe you won't. Remind yourself of the learning process; all of the things you can now do, you definitely couldn't do when you first started learning. Commit yourself to just one month of this new activity. At the end of the month, maybe that will be that – an experience to be pursued no further – but maybe it won't. Push the boundaries of your comfort zone a little bit and maybe soon you too will find yourself as a Salsa dancing, Kung Fu kicking, and arrow-slinging yogi, who also finds time to coach golf. I can assure you the stories and experiences you gain from your own new areas will be well worth it.

Crossing one from the bucket list. The world's highest tandem skydive: 18,000 feet above the Kennedy Space Centre, Orlando, Florida, United States

Lesson #35

Scam lessons

On a recent day off, I was walking around People's Square when I saw a lost-looking foreigner about to be scammed. The tea house scam is a common one; a group ask you to take a photo, act friendly, and then invite you to a teahouse where drink prices are massively inflated, and you are forced to pay the equivalent of several hundred pounds. This man was a fair way through this scam as I walked past, and after thinking for a few seconds I realised I had to stop. I turned, caught the eyes of some members of the group, who definitely looked dodgy, then approached and warned the foreigner about what I thought was going on. I was obviously right, as the angry reaction of the scammers wasn't in line with a legitimate group of tourists wanting a photo taken!

What followed was a tirade of racist abuse; I was called many names, told to go back to my country, and more. Fortunately, the combination of my anger, puffed out chest, death stare and refusal to back down obviously worked, as they eventually wandered off, whilst still giving me abuse for being black, African, Caribbean, a foreigner, short, and muscular. I found the last two insults particularly amusing, as I'm taller than the average Chinese man, including every single one of this group of conmen. Anyway, all's well that ends well; the foreigner was grateful, explaining that he'd only moved here two days ago and hadn't heard of the common scam.

The first lesson I learnt from this was that following your instinct is almost always a great idea. Do not talk yourself out of what you know deep down is right; instead, plough ahead and see the benefits. It's hard to ever know the full implications of your actions and what effect they will have, but being true to what you believe is always a great starting point.

The second lesson, which I only realised retrospectively, is related to how much you can individually control. The following week, a friend and I were walking past the same area when I saw the same group talking to three or four foreigners. They glared at me, and started gesturing and heading towards me. Maybe it was the fact I had just eaten, or that myself and the girl I was with weren't in the best position to face up to seven angry guys, but in this instance I realised I had to accept defeat and walk away. Instead, I took a picture later and shared it online to hopefully raise awareness. Maybe I cannot singlehandedly solve this scam, but I must take some pride in having helped one person out and hope that, as a result, a little good comes from my actions, without the expense of my safety.

Action: Spend today being consciously aware of your natural instincts and trust them. That offer you really want to say no to, but are afraid to, or that potential new friend you walk past on the street but don't have the courage to stop and speak to; make it different today and see where it leads you. At the same time, accept that you can't control or change everything, but take great pride in what little you can.

Lesson #36

Being there vs. being there

I'm now eight months into my China journey, and two of my best friends have just left after a short visit to this side of the world. I lived with these two throughout university, and we share a similar zest for life and desire to live it to the absolute fullest. They're people who know me as well as anyone in the world, so it was awesome for them to see what this phase of my life consists of, as well as how I've developed while being out here. Hearing their news of adventures, travels, work and careers was exciting, and spending holiday time in China with great friends from England was always going to be special.

We've always been able to have fun doing just about anything; when I think back to hilarious evenings at University, doing mundane things like food shopping or washing up, we always had great times. As a result, I had no doubt that time together in China was going to be full of highlights.

Our first couple of days included a cramped, eventful train journey to Xi'an, donning traditional Chinese hats, collectively bowing at the many people we met, and generally being jokers. We were the subject of many photos and made our way into plenty more. We watched traditional (but terrible!) shows at the theatre, made friends on the street, explored new areas, had a fun 16 kilometre cycle around the city wall, and tried to create as many ridiculous photos as possible. We had an awesome time and made many more fantastic memories.

We also visited the Terracotta warriors, a very special and monumental attraction; however, what we saw was a little saddening. We took a lot of time to ask our guide questions, wanting to fully immerse ourselves, to understand some history, and try to comprehend how and why this place came about. What we saw from those around us though was very different. It appeared many tourists were only there to snap a few samey photos, experience nothing, and move on to the next sight. It seemed as if, for them, being there was just a necessity to tick off, so you could say 'done that', before moving on.

If you cannot feel awe in a place as significant as this, I wonder what it would take to grab your attention and give you the satisfaction of having really experienced something amazing. So many moments of magic must be lost through this list-ticking approach to travel. If we want to live life to the absolute fullest, and keep creating memorable moments, this is something to be avoided. We also left with plenty of pictures but what I really want is to hear their stories, to see their faces light up as they tell me about their best experiences. This is simply not possible if you aren't present enough to appreciate the many feelings and experiences that are all around you at each moment.

Action: Your challenge today is to live all of it with a heightened awareness of each moment, as it is the only instance of it you will ever have. Every time you notice your thinking rushing to a past event, or your imagination jumping forward to some task or event coming up, STOP. Pause, look at the world around you, and appreciate it. The sights, smells, sounds, feelings and company are all that matter for now. Get lost in the magic of each and every moment that you're fortunate to be alive, well and functioning, and watch what it can do for your life.

CHINESE REALISATION OF THE DAY

Some Chinese girls are pretty bluntly harsh. I'm at a new Bachata class today, desperately trying to get to a level I'm happy with, as the feeling of being average at best is hurting me. Most people are full of fun and we joke around as we all try to improve. As we switch partners, the typical flirty conversation starts from the new partner. Only this one goes very differently... After a big smile and asking me if I'd been dancing long, she then asks what country I'm from. I say England, and she says (direct quote): "oh, so that's why you can't dance at all!" Straight face. No joke. I let out a shocked laugh and am not sure what to say, so on the next turn, I "forget" to reconnect and leave her alone as I choose my next partner. Wow. Ouch. At that moment, I realised my career as a Bachata dancer was maybe over. Damn my Englishness...

CHINESE REALISATION OF THE DAY

Tai Chi is an easy way to make yourself look stupid. After Tango, Bachata and Salsa lessons this week, alongside laser quest and Chinese lessons, I wanted to try one more thing. Unfortunately, taking a free introduction to Tai Chi class on the same day that a master of Tai Chi has 30 of his long-term (20 years+) students over from Europe wasn't the best idea. Not sure I've ever felt so stared at – particularly by one guy, who couldn't believe I kept mistaking my left foot for my right foot and pointing my hands in the wrong direction whilst trying to follow in the mirror. Tai Chi is crossed off the list of new activities, not sure it will become a habit though!

CHINESE REALISATION OF THE DAY

Public, physical contact with a Westerner may be very embarrassing for a Chinese lady. Last night I carried on the theme of new experiences and, with a few friends, took an introductory Tango class. When the partners were switched up after a few minutes we were also told that the lady had to put her hands on the guy's chest for the starting position. I've never seen anyone go SO red as quickly as my mid-20-year-old Chinese partner did right then as she fumbled her hands onto my chest. In fairness, she settled into it and seemed to be enjoying it just a few moments later!

CHINESE REALISATION OF THE DAY

Public nudity and Chinese men equals extreme embarrassment. So, a Russian woman in the Bachata class today was wearing a very low cut top, which, combined with ambitiously enthusiastic dancing, led to her boobs falling out of said top. In the dark lights and crowded room, this could have easily gone unnoticed. However, the tall lady (also wearing heels), who dwarfed her Chinese dance partner, had quite a lot of attention drawn to her by his hilarious attempts to comically avoid looking at what was RIGHT in his face. The look of embarrassment on his face was unreal and to make it even better (or worse!), she was so vacantly dancing and busy avoiding looking at him through the dance that nobody noticed for at least a few minutes...

CHINESE REALISATION OF THE DAY

Be wary of Chinese hats. After a few tourist days with great friends from England, wearing traditional Chinese field workers hats and getting many inquisitive looks, smiles, waves and pictures taken, we decided to take the 16 kilometre bike ride around Xi'an city wall. All was going well until literally the last 200 metres when we had a race to the line... Going as fast as you can, plus wind, equals hat in the face, which means no vision. A scary few seconds followed as I could see absolutely nothing, tried to brake, and then went flying over the handlebars which ended in a smashed screen, bent/broken phone, hurt pride, another ridiculous story, and fortunately nothing more than a bit of wrist pain and swollen fingers. Hmmmm.

Terracotta Warriors, Xi'an – buried over 2000 years ago and only discovered by accident in 1974

A visit to China without belting it out at KTV would just not be right...

Lesson #37

What turns you on?

Within the last week I've been fortunate enough to meet a wonderful new friend and Salsa teacher, who I've spent a lot of time chatting to, getting to know her and what makes her tick. Through listening a lot, asking plenty of questions, and offering any advice I felt my life experiences could warrant, I was able to ease some of her doubts, broaden her horizons, and make a few things a bit clearer – ultimately helping her a teeny bit in making a huge decision that will affect her future. Being able to give a little, and see the potential impact it could have on her life, was incredibly humbling and satisfying for me.

A while ago, I was talking to a friend who asked me what I really wanted to do with my life. I imagined my passion for golf, and the fact I'd just graduated with a degree in Applied Golf Management Studies, might have something to do with it! I also knew I had a strong desire to travel, meet new people, explore new cultures, and have a lot of fun. Several months later, those dreams led to me working as a golf coach while travelling the world on a cruise ship, stopping off at some 30 countries around the world over the course of 100 days. Later still, they've led me to many more countries, including my current stage in Shanghai.

I still often reflect on that question though, and only now am I starting to see my real answer. I want to challenge you to do the same. The closer you get, and the more accurate your answer, the more time you will spend being able to do those things you really want to achieve.

On the surface, it might appear that coaching golf is my absolute passion, and I'd be lying if I told you I didn't get a huge buzz from watching someone transform their confidence, become vastly more competent, reach their goals, and enjoy themselves playing golf. I am now realising though, from digging down much deeper, that what really gets me going is something deeper than that. If golf ceased to exist tomorrow, I would still be able to fulfil my calling, I am sure.

Let me explain: What really excites me is to ability to serve others and put their needs above my own.

Coaching with two of my young superstars

Action: Have a think, a real think. Turn the light off, switch the Internet off, and ask yourself a few questions. What's been the happiest moment in your last three months? What really excites you? I guarantee the deeper you can delve down into these answers, the more opportunities you will find that enable you to spend time in the areas that excite you most, and be able to use your unique skills to yours and others' benefits.

Lesson #38

Being busy

I have always been the kind of person who has a lot of things going on at once. I have friends all around the world, and keeping up with the interesting things they're all up to could be a full time job. When you add that to coaching golf, researching to improve my coaching skills, exploring and having adventures in my new city, spending time on social media, writing, relaxing, trying new things, learning new skills, having a social life, exercise, and occasionally sleeping, I often wonder how I find enough time to do it all.

Time in China has, however, helped me realise more and more that I need to prioritise or I will burn out.

Fortunately, I have many wise and experienced mentors around me, who help and guide me, and often help me to realise before it's too late, so I'm happy to say I've so far managed to avoid reaching that point.

Life will always be busy, there will always be too many things to do, and if you keep waiting for the day when everything can be achieved, it just won't happen. Prioritise or burn out. I hear many people telling me, almost as if it's a badge of honour, how busy they are, and that there isn't enough time to get everything done. If you look at my list of open internet tabs, bookmarks and saved pages, I could easily feel the same way. Being ever inquisitive, there are a million and one things I'd love to find out more about. However, knowing that there are limited hours in the day means I now spend

Suit + tie? No excuses for not hitting the gym!

my time on the activities that will give me most in return, or that I enjoy the most. Prioritising allows me enough time to choose what else I would like to try having already ticked off the most important things, rather than running behind, playing catch up and feeling busy in order to get back on track.

I've never been one to make excuses. If you want to make something happen then you'd better find the time to make it happen. Also, if something means enough to you then you stand a great chance of making it happen. As a frequent gym-goer – which in China means I'm subject to people constantly squeezing my arms and telling me I am 'very strong' – one of the first things I wanted to do when I moved here was to find a gym. Unfortunately, the local area had a limited choice, so instead I decided to buy my own equipment and create a small home gym, and thus saving preparation and time spent travelling. At the metro station, I also committed to never using the escalator so I am often the only person who makes their way up the stairs, often sprinting or bounding up in an attempt to keep active which has been a good work around. It's quick, easy, fun, and simple to initiate, but has led to a lot of exercise (and even a few saved moments) that could otherwise have been missed.

Action: Look at all the things you want to do with your life, note the top 15 priorities, and try to order them from the most to the least important to you. This could be a list of skills to learn, or where you want to spend time. It could help you realise what skills are most important for you, or that you need to spend more family time. This list is very individual; however, the act of writing it down and having a deep think about what your priorities are will help. For all those things that you'd love to improve at, or perhaps even new skills you'd love to learn, it is unlikely you can give any of them full-time commitment and dedication due to time restraints. However, if you gave it just a few minutes each day, or managed to interweave it within another activity, would you be able to improve over an extended period? If you agree with me, that the answer to this question is yes, the challenge is on. Make a pledge to yourself that each day you will make small progress towards this bigger goal. You'll thank me for it in a few months.

Still got it! Stunning views at Clearwater Bay Golf Course, Hong Kong

Lesson #39

A childlike viewpoint: don't forget the important things

This afternoon I took one of my youngest golfers to the course for the first time. The six-year-old in question is blessed with fantastic parents, whose main goal is to ensure I teach their son many valuable life lessons and help turn him into an even more accomplished, well-rounded person, not just (or even) a great golfer. My goals are obviously in line with theirs, whilst also wanting to keep golf as fun as possible, to ensure he will want to play and improve for the rest of his life, alongside his parents.

Watching his gaze as we pulled in was priceless. Whereas I was instantly preoccupied with seeing how busy the course looked and ensuring our clubs were being taken to the correct place, his eyes glossed over as he admired the golf shop's displays of shiny clubs, colourful clothes, bright gloves and multi-coloured golf balls. His awe only increased when we started walking towards the course itself. Now, all of a sudden, there was a huge lake and fountain; many different types, lengths and colours of grass; twigs and leaves scattered everywhere; the sight of a married couple looking for a lost ball on the adjacent hole; the shouts of 'fore' coming from all around; bits of wooden tees scattered everywhere; and a tiny pot full of grass seed that the caddy kept sprinkling on the ground, to replace his divots and cover our tracks.

For a second, I had to take off my coaching hat and put on my 'life' hat. This young man in front of me was teaching me more than I was teaching him. Golf for him right now is much more than just hitting a small white ball. Instead of just being a measure of how well he played on the course, his experience of the day was much richer. He learnt many new things, created many memories, and discovered new wonders in the world, which would have been very easy to miss completely if he'd had an adult brain in his head.

It is so easy to take things for granted in our everyday life. I personally cannot remember the last time I paid so much attention to the grass on the golf course, or the tweeting of the birds. But, as I listened to him thinking aloud, and resisted the urge to always bring him back to hitting another shot, it was a welcome reminder to enjoy the beauty of the world around me. Even the idea of a golf course, so familiar to me, and so close to the centre of an enormous and developing business city, suddenly wasn't something I could take for granted today, and I left the course with many new perspectives.

Action: Pick five places where you spend a lot of time. Maybe it's your bedroom, your car, your favourite restaurant, or absolutely anywhere else. Try to relax and just 'be' in that place, having as few thoughts in your mind as possible. Pretend this is the very first time you have been in that place, and try to note what comes into your conscious thoughts. Often, we 'know' a situation so well that we take most of it for granted, but try to get back to that childlike wonder and then note down on paper some of the things that are special about these places.

Lesson #40

Make it an experience

Maybe it was because I had just had my busiest coaching month, or maybe it was simply being away from homely familiarity, but the festive period really crept up on me. After a relatively late decision to go away, I found myself travelling to Japan for the first time, to spend Christmas in Tokyo.

Being in Japan for Christmas, away from both England and even my new 'home' in Shanghai, was certainly different. However, I felt that a complete change was much better than simply being away but in a different 'home.'

We decided to skip the 'traditional' KFC meal that has become the national Christmas dish of Japan – apparently it is often ordered months in advance to avoid queues up to two hours long! As an alternative, we debated going to find somewhere serving Western Christmas dinners, however I am glad we didn't in the end. When I think of the ingredients that make up our traditional Christmas dinner, it's interesting to note that, despite being far from a fussy eater, I'm not actually hugely keen on turkey, Brussels sprouts, or even Christmas pudding. Why, therefore, would I want to pay extra money to eat that food out here, when there is no way it would match Mum's cranberry sauce, pigs in blankets, or ice cream Christmas pudding anyway?

It was the whole experience of Christmas at home that I knew I'd miss, not just the individual parts that make it up. I would miss eating the customary annual Brussels sprout, pulling crackers and telling horrendous jokes, catching up with family members, afternoon food coma naps, and watching everybody open their presents. The whole experience of Christmas is what makes it special, and I'm glad I got to Skype home to at least witness some of that.

Instead, I ate probably one of my most expensive meals to date – and man, was it worth it! After stumbling around numerous sushi restaurants, where availability ranged from two month long waiting lists to 'members-only', we were recommended a very highly rated place and, due to being so early for dinner, managed to get a seat. With no set menu and a very classy interior, we weren't massively surprised by the really high prices, but when in Tokyo...right?

What followed was two hours of foodie perfection. Our own personal chef explained every bit of sushi and sashimi as he prepared it, showing where each piece was cut from, alongside much trivia about the restaurant's 130-year history, different recipes, where fish is sourced, and his journey and inspirations as a sushi chef. The venue was very welcoming and, despite it being so high-end, we felt comfortable – even taking a million and one pictures of everything. All of the chefs would add in stories between making their food, and they all had a genuine love for their work, which was exciting to witness. AND. THE. FOOD... Wow.

I genuinely will struggle to enjoy any other sushi again after that experience. Every combination of flavours was perfect, and each morsel was prepared as a visual masterpiece. The freshness was incredible. Previously average sushi pieces were somehow transformed into works of art, and a look of awe and constant wonder did not leave my face for the whole two hours.

Despite the price, the whole spectacle of the event made it more than worth it, and reinforced a valuable lesson: "under promise and over deliver" – or, even better still, "promise and over deliver." Whether it's in the business world or even personal relationships, be known as the person who always exceeds expectations and you too will be as successful as a restaurant that can survive in the sushi capital of the world for over 130 years!

Action: If you think back to a great holiday or event that you were a part of, it is often the small touches added together that lead to a fantastic all-round experience. For the next week, in one situation each day, think of how you can over deliver on something you have promised. Go out of your way to provide a service or experience that exceeds what is expected, and make a note of the reactions you receive.

Sushiko Honten – a master sushi chef at work and an end product ALMOST too good looking to eat!

CHINESE REALISATION OF THE DAY

Chinese people don't like cosying up with foreigners on the metro. This is an almost daily occurrence. Watching the local guy or girl squeeze in between the other seven people on the other side of the carriage, making them all cosy up, move luggage, and basically sit in each other's lap. At the same time, with one foreigner on my side of the carriage, there is never even an attempt to get any more than five people seated! Maybe my use of deodorant has the opposite effect here than it has back home…

CHINESE REALISATION OF THE DAY

If you want some signature practice, lose your bank card and attempt to get a replacement. I lost count at 13 but I'm sure, in the last hour or so, I've signed my name at least 20 times for the simple process of getting a new card and changing some currency. What do they do with all of those signed sheets and passport page photocopies?!

CHINESE REALISATION OF THE DAY

Anger doesn't last long in China. I'm at the busiest metro station, and many people are waiting to get on and off the metro. The people are queuing more 'English-like' than normal, apart from one lady. I gesture to her to get out of the way of the people getting off, so she does with a scowl, and the people get off. On the train she looks at me again, tries to scowl, and then there's a priceless moment as she looks at me, seemingly forgets her mood, bursts into a smile and anger is diffused. Not happy with that, she then tries the scowl again. I'm not sure if my surprised and confused laugh straight at her made her feel less angry or not!

Not quite what you expect to see in a bag on the metro escalator!

CHINESE REALISATION OF THE DAY

There is never a dull moment. Expect the unexpected. I finish my dance lesson and I am coming home on the metro. I get slightly confused as I see that the guy in front of me is carrying what looks like a goat in a suitcase bag. He comically keeps colliding with everything as he goes past, so I snap a few pictures. I then get out of the metro to be met by four or five of the regular taxi drivers who literally start singing "Obama, Obama" as I come out!

CHINESE REALISATION OF THE DAY

The awareness of personal space gene was left out of a few people here. I am in the metro and walking towards me was a man, who out of nowhere, in the middle of the walkway, bent down to tie up his shoe. This would be fine, except it was pretty busy. The person directly behind was too late to realise and banged into him and cringily held his waist as he stumbled. Then, the lady behind (on her phone of course) also walked into the pair before another older man managed to narrowly avoid getting caught up in the mess. I think it was only my extra loud laugh that stopped anyone else joining the pile up as I walked by!

Lesson #41

Thinking outside the box

After an unusual Christmas and Boxing Day that didn't feel hugely festive, today I decided to escape the Tokyo bustle and walk up Mount Takao, a 600-metre small mountain not far out of central Tokyo. I viewed this as a great way to exercise and escape the busyness, as well as enjoying unparalleled views of Mount Fuji and out towards the city. I chose what is supposedly the hardest route, which promised waterfalls, a Buddhist temple, streams, and wildlife. A leisurely stroll, stopping along the way to take some pictures and enjoy the stillness, got me to the top in time for lunch. After eating, and once again being amazed by how few bins there are in Tokyo, I put my rubbish in my bag and started the easier walk back down.

Around halfway down I came to the steepest part, which fortunately was paved. The road was wide and quiet so I tried something different just for fun. I had been finding that, despite the incline, it wasn't any easier to gain speed walking down normally. Something to do with how high you could lift your leg, and therefore the length of your stride, meant that not only did it not feel great on your knee but it also wasn't particularly fast.

Instead, I turned around and started walking backwards down the hill, and it felt like I was flying! The stride length was massively increased and, before long, I was receiving a few strange looks but also travelling much further without much effort at all. I later did a little test and worked out I was gaining an extra two steps for every eight I was walking; not a bad result. I must have looked quite funny in my casual clothes as I whizzed past experienced walkers with their walking sticks, specialised shoes and clothing; however, to my amusement (and it was easy to see, as I was facing the right way!) the people behind me started experimenting and copying what I was doing. I spotted five people walking backwards, trialling it, and then continuing to walk that way. It was certainly more efficient, and a fun way to see all that was around you as well.

Many great inventions came about due to curiosity and creative problem solving. Often the result seems so obvious, but it took somebody thinking outside of the box to come up with the idea in the first place. If you follow what has always been done, you will get the same results you always have. Is this what you want – or do you want the absolute best?

When you start to think this way, you realise the potential awesomeness out there. It was a little written brainstorm, which showed I loved golf, travel and new adventures that first put the idea of teaching golf on a cruise ship in my mind. A few months later and I was on board a 100-day world cruise, working as a golf professional. There I met somebody who had loved going on a cruise so much that he'd wanted to get involved. He had a desire to travel, but could only speak English, didn't want to work in hospitality, had a limited skill set (his words!) and little performing experience – so he became a puppeteer and travels round the world on-board a cruise ship, language skills not required!

Action: Write down a number of things that you spend time doing or that you'd like to achieve. Imagine there is nothing holding you back and you have unlimited creativity and opportunities. What could you do to better move towards these goals? How could you combine multiple passions to bridge the gap between work and play? How could you discover how to descend the road faster? Giving time to realise and improve how you deal with certain situations will, I'm sure, have many benefits – and don't be surprised if you shock yourself at how things can turn out when you think outside of the box.

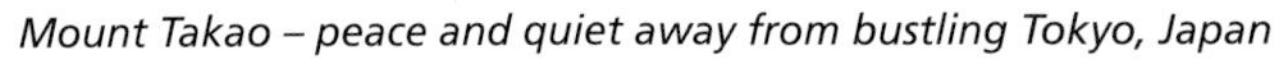
Mount Takao – peace and quiet away from bustling Tokyo, Japan

Lesson #42

Is the grass always greener?

Every time I leave Shanghai, it's easy to make comparisons and conclude that, the new place is "better."

On my first Hong Kong trip, I was very tempted to film myself leaving the MTR, as I was so stunned that the people there actually waited until after I'd left to get onto the vehicle. This sounds ridiculous, but more than once in Shanghai, when wanting to leave and seeing people stood blocking my exit, I have had to barge them back a few steps backwards in a mini rugby tackle!

In Hong Kong also I've also noticed far fewer people spitting in the street, and there's less of a feeling that you're in the minority of people who don't smoke. There are stores that sell all the toiletries and other oddities you hadn't even realised you missed from England – plus a huge number of Western stores, including Marks and Spencer that stock my favourite sweets.

Similarly, on arrival in Tokyo, I spent the first day in honeymoon mode. Everything was glossy, new and exciting, with crystal blue skies, and I spent time in a stunning, enormous national park in the city centre. The internet speed was faster than in Shanghai, and I didn't have the hassle of requiring a VPN, as I usually do to bypass the Chinese firewalls. Compared to my list of dislikes about Shanghai, which includes the pollution, lack of open spaces and nature, not speaking the language, restricted internet access, and being miles from home, it seemed quite logical to believe that maybe moving to Tokyo would be a better choice. All it proved, however, is how little I really knew my own thoughts about what really an important effect on my contentment with where I am has; by the end of the week I was able to emphatically confirm that I am so glad to live in Shanghai.

My boss passed on something he was told prior to arriving eleven years ago; as time goes on, it gets truer: "To work in, Shanghai is the best; whereas other nearby places are great to travel to and explore on holidays."

I've since written a list of great things Shanghai has. As my list grew, it amazed me that I had already started to take for granted so many of the things I love about my current home. With this realisation and subsequent renewed appreciation, I could look at the same situations and feel grateful, knowing that I'm in exactly the right place for me right now.

High up on that list was how exciting it is to be in a place that's right in the middle of such rapid expansion. This fact means that in this incredibly international city, on an almost daily basis I meet ridiculously interesting people, who are doing a huge variety of things – starting their own businesses and much more. It's this variety that I'm sure would be less common in many other locations. I'll take life in Shanghai, without a doubt; I've realised you cannot exclaim that the grass is always greener on the other side, unless you notice how green it is on your side first.

Action: Observing what really makes you happy means that it will be a lot easier to replicate and find yourself in those situations again. This week, start work on an extended challenge to write down a list of 100 things in life that you are grateful for.

Think about things that make you happy, such as taking time out in a place that's meaningful to you, a phone call to a friend, or being able to donate to charity through your time and money. Perhaps it's leaving a surprise for somebody special to you, or learning a new skill. Putting thoughts down on paper can help solidify the sentiment and also means you're in a far more reasonable place to compare situations, rather than always deciding it's what you don't have, or what is out of reach, that would somehow make everything in the world perfect. After being in China, I know that when I return to England for visits there will be many things on that list I wasn't previously thankful for. Clean air, people speaking the same language, and familiar culture are things it's easy to take for granted when they're all around you. For that reason, think deeply and note down how you feel as you look down at a list of 100 things you have in your life right now that you are grateful for.

Shinjuku Gyoen National Garden (above), and Mount Fiji (below), Tokyo, Japan

Lesson #43

Everything happens in 'China time'

In the rush of getting back to China after a recent trip, I forgot to go and check in with the police to re-register. As I remember it there was a lot going on, and finding my feet and some good local food happened instead! As a result, several weeks later, I finally made it along to the police station with the HR woman from my work to register as being in the country. Thankfully, I wasn't deported and was able to escape with just a warning.

The visit started well, with an easy chat with the first officer at the station before being told to wait in line. Unfortunately, moving on took another hour before I was ushered upstairs, where the fun and games really began. After taking my passport, the officer spent the next 90 minutes investigating it, asking questions, and laboriously transferring all of my passport data onto the computer. Throughout this, I had to sit waiting, and waiting, before waiting a little more. Every 20 minutes or so, the officer would hold the passport picture up and confirm my likeness before continuing to scour through the pages, inspecting my multiple visas and arrivals stamps. Amusingly, after all of this, in an attempt at small talk as we walked downstairs for the final phase of the procedure, the same officer asked me if I was American. Apparently the 90 minutes he'd spent looking through my passport weren't enough for him to find out my nationality!

As the time ticked on, I could have become increasingly annoyed. Given I was already the one in the wrong, however, I suspected those in charge of the situation wouldn't have taken too kindly to that. Instead, I spent the majority of my time in the station learning some Chinese with the HR girl who'd accompanied me. The same amount of time still passed but, to me, it felt like a valuable few hours and reminded me of a lesson I've been taught many times over the course of my time playing golf. I used to get annoyed whenever the weather was windy and affected my game. Years later, I eventually accepted that everyone on the course was facing the same conditions, and I'd give myself a significant advantage if I could just learn to love the wind and climb ahead of those bemoaning the bad weather.

As I'm now approaching the end of my first year in China, I've seen all the seasons and the many challenges that different times of the year bring. I've witnessed ridiculous holiday times when every person, nationwide, is given the same week off work, causing a near meltdown on public transport and making the idea of travel ludicrous. I've managed to survive the month or so when my patience was tested and I wondered daily what exactly made me irresistibly tasty to so many mosquitos. I coped when flies would swarm around the house, entering through small cracks around the windows if there was even the slightest sign of food on display. I endured the times when pollution was so high the government suggested you stay indoors, and the city disappeared in a mist. I sweated through several months, when the thought of being without air-conditioning for even a moment was scary. I must have annoyed my cleaner no end with the ridiculous amount of clothing I would get through during each of those sweltering weeks, and yet all of that seems a million miles away.

Now it is winter and I'm realising that my poor circulation means even three pairs of trousers, four tops, three pairs of socks, gloves, a woolly hat and neck warmer will only just about allow me to function outside for longer than five minutes.

As I reflect on all these season and times, I have to laugh. At the time, all these issues seemed like such huge events. I remember particularly being at the end of my tether as I applied a mix of insect repellent sprays, creams, lotions and more, whilst wrapping up tightly under my duvet, and still being awoken several hours later, ridden with itchy mosquito bites. However on reflection, other than a few funny stories, all these less than ideal situations have long since faded to the back of my mind. On the whole, I would say the living conditions have been great and have hardly stopped me from enjoying my life and work to the fullest. Much of the 'pain' is now forgotten, which begs the question: was it really such a big deal in the first place?

I've made sure throughout it all to focus my attention on what my first golf coach labelled the 'controllables', instead of expending energy, time and frustration on things I can't control. I can control how I deal with events, making the best of frustrating situations, avoiding travel at certain times, wearing appropriate clothes for all seasons, and working out the best way to control insect invasions. Likewise, I can stay my happy self and not get bogged down by the million and one uncontrollable things that have great power to potentially affect my mood.

Action: Take a notebook with you as you go about your life today. Note down any moments that make you upset, angry, cross, or agitated. Perhaps the long queue in the supermarket or the fact that the weather meant you had to cancel your evening plans. At the end of the day, highlight in yellow the 'controllable' and in red the 'uncontrollable.' Write down potential solutions to each 'controllable' annoyance and then get creative about how you could deal best with the 'uncontrollable.' Often, having visible proof of how much we worry about the things outside of our control is enough to help us make a change and, instead, only use our finite attention to tune into things that can actually enhance our experience of life.

Minus 15 degrees in Harbin, Heilongjiang, China's Northernmost major city, but the sights of the biggest Ice Festival in the world more than made up for it

Lesson #44

What would future you say?

I'm currently sat in a taxi, more than a little disappointed to be leaving the rest of the academy team, as well as around 100 others from the company and our investors, midway through dinner at the two-day annual work party.

I'm flying to Vietnam for a holiday in the morning, and being four hours drive away from Shanghai meant that getting back on the last train, packing and then resting for my flight was not only a priority but also the only option, as no taxi drivers seemed to fancy the eight-hour round trip. My 90-minute taxi ride will be followed by a break, and then a further 90 minutes on the train; all of this after only having completed the three and a half hour drive to get to the party about five hours previously. On paper, this may seem like a lot of hassle for that amount of time (agreed!) but actually, in retrospect, I wouldn't have had it any other way.

Today has been a slightly surreal day. The long outward journey was finished with a traditional Chinese lunch, before climbing up a mountain to complete various photo challenges. The afternoon consisted of a mix of random games, extremely enthusiastic competitors, ridiculous fails, many photos, and lots of laughing. It was great to see the rest of our academy team outside the work environment, and to team build a little in this way. As usual, I spent a fair chunk of it acting the fool and finding ways to practise my Chinese with the many new people I met. We witnessed some beautiful views, watched a local make life-endangering attempts at retrieving vegetables from a very steep portion of the mountain, with no harness or protection, and enjoyed lots of other new experiences.

When I think of today, it reminds me of what is really important: creating experiences, memories, and personal contact, through developing new and stronger friendships. It would have been very easy to miss out completely on today, and decide it wasn't worth the hassle, but I'm glad I didn't.

I recently re-watched the videos from my skydive in Orlando and my bungee jumps in Auckland and, more recently, from the Macau Tower. At the time, the decision to pay extra for the videos was more financially difficult that it would be now, but in retrospect it was so worth it to have a lifetime souvenir of some of the ridiculous faces I pulled, and to be able to relive the experience. Quite often, what seems like a huge problem at the time will not even be 'a thing' at all as time goes by. Previously I could only imagine whether this day of randomness with my colleagues would be worth the hassle of all this extra travel, but I'm pretty sure I made the right decision in the end.

Action: Whenever you're thinking about a decision, ask yourself what the 'future you' would say in a few months or even years. This could also be related to taking action in a task, deciding whether or not to carry on an argument that could be ended and moved on from, saying yes to something that will require a little more effort, or even saying no to something that you really do not want to commit to.

HONG KONG REALISATION OF THE DAY

Apparently in Hong Kong, there is NOTHING that a local will not stop doing if she or he sees a lost looking group of friendly foreigners nearby. Yesterday people interrupted dates, phone calls, conversations and reading books just to pop open Google maps and give me a bit of help if they could.

CHINESE REALISATION OF THE DAY

You always have to think through the pros and cons of each decision here! On reflection, I'm not entirely sure the mad run to get through the closing doors of the metro was worth it. Yes, I did save four minutes by not missing the train and yes, I did feel quite satisfied at having made it. On the other hand, the disapproving glances that lasted at least three stops from the family of the old lady I accidentally semi-groped in my rush onto the train were not ideal. On the plus side, the 70+ year-old in question found this all hilarious, and kept glancing over and smiling!

CHINESE REALISATION OF THE DAY

Either I am reading into things too much, or there are some very sneaky Chinese people around the place. I was out for dinner with two friends last night, and the place started to close down pretty early by Shanghai standards. At around 9.30pm, the lights are switched low, music stops and everything starts getting closed off. Fast forward to 10pm, and the other remaining table goes to leave. Next, Mr Manager comes close and 'The Final Countdown' is played on his phone like a ringtone; he leaves it, it "rings" for around 30 seconds, before we get the hint and start to leave. Priceless!

CHINESE REALISATION OF THE DAY

Listen carefully to what people say to avoid silly miscommunication. In the shopping centre I ask a helpful looking employee, in Chinese, where the toilet is. She responded like she was saying "hello" in a strange accent...so I smiled and asked again. This happened 3x and each time I'm finding her apparent attempt at an English accent funny. It's only on the 4th time when she gestured with her hand upwards that I clocked that she was indeed saying 'èr lóu' or second floor in Chinese...

CHINESE REALISATION OF THE DAY

Whatever seems logical to you, think the opposite and you might be close to predicting some of the situations here. In the two minutes I was watching this guy repairing wires, in the middle of a busy crossing, in the middle of rush hour(!), he was almost knocked down three times and of course, he was not wearing a helmet!

Rush hour, surely the best time to go about fixing a cable on a busy road...

Lesson #45

Crossing the road

I'm in Ho Chi Minh City, Vietnam and cannot believe the number of motorbikes. I thought Shanghai had an abundance of people whizzing along roads, walkways and garden paths on their mechanical contraptions, but that was nothing compared to this. At last count, there were two million scooters here, but the petrol equivalent is faster and larger, making them more daunting... and much louder. The level of skill required to ride one and avoid collisions on a minute-by-minute basis is therefore exponentially higher. My hat goes off (definitely not my helmet, that is staying on!) to those who manage daily to get from A to B safely on one of those things. Perhaps due to the extra attention the drivers take, I only saw one accident all week and, other than a lot of honking and beeping, wouldn't have thought many more were on the horizon either.

As with most of the Asian countries I've visited, traffic rules are relaxed to say the least. Green and red lights often don't correlate to any kind of action. With so many motorists, hectic roads, and visitors, it could be a recipe for disaster. Hilariously, you quickly start to see who has been in the city a while and for whom it is still their 'breaking in' period. The rookies attempt to cross, hesitate as a car or motorbike approaches, and often spend several minutes edging forward and back, confusing motorists and causing lots of swerving. The 'old hand' arrogantly walks at a constant pace, hardly looking at the traffic as road users adapt and avoid, and very soon reach the other side of the road. Simple.

On Vietnamese roads, and in life, you can fritter away so much time if you are second guessing every decision, talking yourself out of things, seeking too many opinions, and just not taking action. This is normal. However, don't be afraid to move out of your comfort zone; some of life's best experiences occur only after you venture out. If your instinct told you that a decision was a 'goer' before you enlisted the contrasting opinions of 78,329 others, I believe that is enough to justify at least attempting and discovering for yourself, instead of backing away. Once you have that inkling, try to get to the action phase quickly, before you have time to evaluate everything to the nth degree. If I scrutinised absolutely everything in life, I don't think I would ever get out of the house for deliberating the choice of what to have for breakfast!

This kind of thinking will definitely help you get to the other side of the road much faster, instead of walking on the spot. Fortunately for me, I turned into a Vietnamese road-crossing 'old hand' quite quickly and, I'm happy to report, I survived my stay.

I have though had more personal mishaps this year than anywhere before. Despite surviving the Vietnamese traffic, my time in Asia has seen possessions misplaced, headphones broken in a ridiculous scuffle, smashed phones, lost cards, car crashes, ludicrous injuries and more.

Leaving my electric scooter in the back of a Shanghai taxi recently was a particular lowlight. I searched and searched for something positive to take from the fact I'd effectively thrown a lot of (uninsured) money out of the window. It was tough, especially as the actual loss and the lack of insurance were all my fault. As I write this, the lyrics "there's no mistakes in life ever, it's only lessons" play in my ear, which is ironic, but perhaps also further evidence of why this time to reflect has been useful.

I had delayed getting contents insurance and also getting a GPS chip put inside my scooter, which would have helped me track it. On both of these points, I knew I needed to take action; however, that action was never taken. Instead, I put it off, only to be revisited when it was actually too late. Both of these actions have been rectified now, and fortunately I learnt this lesson in a situation that 'only' cost me a few hundred pounds, rather than one where much more could have been at stake.

Action: Whilst I wouldn't directly recommend reckless living, or not consulting others before crossing your own roads and making big decisions, I would recommend taking action sooner rather than later. Make it a conscious choice to listen to what you believe is a good idea; don't weaken your resolve through constant questioning of your decision, and push yourself out of your comfort zone as you cross to the other side of that road. Note down some of these decisions and your initial thoughts on the subject and then, over time, collate the results to see how things turned out. This will give you even more confidence in the results you see.

Making it 2,000,001 scooters on the roads of Ho Chi Minh City, Vietnam!

The world's highest commercial bungee jump, 233 metres up on the Macau Tower. The autonomous territory of Macau is on the southern coast of China, 60 kilometres west of Hong Kong.

Lesson #46

Jumping regrets

Today was spent in Dalat, a 300 kilometre drive north east of Ho Chi Minh City, climbing through and abseiling down waterfalls, sliding down rocks, hiking, wading through rivers, and diving from cliffs into pools of crystal clear waters. As an adrenaline lover, this was awesome. The opportunity to witness new things, see unparalleled beauty of nature, meet new people, and push my boundaries a little bit are ingredients for a great day

Although the skill set wasn't especially difficult, unlike my bungee jumps and skydives, there was far more learned technique involved, which added to my excitement and nervousness. There was assistance if you made a mistake and slipped, but the idea of falling and having 25 metres between you and jagged rock, with just a few ropes for safety, still wasn't appealing.

It was interesting, within our group of 11, to see the differences in confidence levels, fears, comfort zones, and boundaries. We were a mix of younger and older thrill-seekers, ranging from lone, young and eager travellers to older married couples, and everything in between – each with more than a few screws loose to consider choosing and paying to spend a day doing this! From the dry runs and water slides, to the water abseiling and plunging into what is labelled "the washing machine", I was one of three to complete every activity. I may have come across as someone without fears and with nerves of steel, but I'd label myself more as someone who had trust in the equipment and staff who were guiding us, and who doesn't like regrets. This is something I like to live by in all areas of my life, hence taking the giant leap to move out to China in the first place.

Everyone is wired differently, and previous experiences, current feelings and prior exposure led to individual differences in how much people were able to do during the day. Whereas, for some, the idea of jumping 15 metres into water below is OK, for others the limit may be just one metre, and for others 35 metres sounds just fine. Today many of the team pushed themselves far beyond their comfort zones, and watching their reactions as they succeeded and conquered their fear was fun. Guys and girls who were initially reluctant softened as they saw each person before them succeed, and watching them want to repeat the action after initially overcoming their hurdle was incredible to observe.

Knowing your own limits is vital. I am definitely not wired for some of the death-defying stunts I have watched in YouTube videos, but I know when to push my limits and ensure I don't live with regret for not doing something I wanted to experience. This kind of thinking helps make you proud of what you have achieved and provides you with some awesome memories, as well as an enhanced belief about what you can accomplish when you put your mind to it, which is always useful!

Action: Do something each day for the next seven days that scares you. These could be planned in advance, or spontaneously taking a risk you normally wouldn't. It could mean asking 'that' girl out on a date, reaching out and contacting an expert in your field for advice, trying a new club or activity that you've been putting off for a while. I've done all these and many more things that scared me at the time, but ultimately been very happy with the results. Challenge on!

Lesson #47

Do it, and do it well

When I was younger, I wanted to be a dinosaur. I also wanted to be a carpenter and a fireman, before these turned into more selfish ideas of wanting to be a world famous actor or footballer. Eventually, that dream turned into wanting to be the best golfer I could possibly be.

I spent many hours improving, competing and studying, before realising that the satisfaction I got from coaching was far greater than the satisfaction that I got from playing and that, realistically, I likely wasn't good enough to make a career from playing competitive golf. The fact I could become a golf coach while still enjoying the amazing variety of life – travelling the world, meeting new people, sharing my knowledge, and making people's lives better – made this a dream job for me.

In the last few days, while I've been in Vietnam, I've seen many people also living out their dream jobs.

When you think of a perfect job, what do you imagine? Big salaries? Lavish houses? Fame? Endless holidays? Well, the dream jobs I've seen here have ranged from a tour guide to a hotel owner, and a street artist to a cleaner.

First, what is a dream job? That definition, of course, will vary from person to person, and I'm sure even from day to day; but for me, it's about variety, being satisfied with knowing you're making a small difference to the world, human interaction and an opportunity to smile, and always having new challenges that ensure boredom never sets in. Those are all the things I'd be looking for in a dream job, and all the Vietnamese jobs listed above definitely provided those.

These people certainly loved what they did and you could really sense their desire to be the absolute best at the job they had. Passion shone through in everything they did, and it was infectious just from spending time with them. I'm sure it would be possible to find a more glamorous and well-paid job than many of them, but the genuine smiles these people gave me as we interacted told me they wouldn't change it for the world.

There's a quote I hear all of the time, which says: 'if you do a job you love, you'll never have to work another day in your life'. Our hotel manager in Ho Chi Minh City definitely embodied this; the pleasure she got from being able to recommend and help organise trips was incredible, and the joy on her face when we reported back with our positive experiences was even better. She, I would say, has a dream job: she shares smiles, helps others, is around people, has variety each day, and makes a difference to the experiences of tourists. Quite different from what I would have labelled as a perfect job before!

It's got me thinking of the stories about Bill Gates at the current stage in his career, having earned billions of dollars yet now gaining satisfaction from being able to give lots of it away. In no way am I suggesting that having money is a bad thing, and of course many of my adventures have required money, but being fully aware of what brings happiness in your life is very valuable in a more significant way.

Happiness comes from inside. Many of the happiest people I've met have been amongst the poorest and least fortunate, left in situations that definitely could warrant self-pity and frustration. Instead, smiles never left their faces and they were grateful for every blessing. Likewise, I've also spent time in blissful, lavish, wealthy settings and seen miserable people. Our scenarios and external situations do not define us or give us happiness and sadness. The illusion that we will be happy 'when' something else happens puts the power of our own feelings out of reach – never a good idea!

I've felt my happiest and fulfilled when in the presence of great family and friends, helping others, or often when doing very little at all, allowing my mind to focus solely on whatever's in front of me, rather than thinking of a million and one different things at once. I've learnt that you can lead the lifestyle of a millionaire, and achieve the happiness I thought these external factors would provide, without having even a fraction of the money or 'things.'

Action: Your job is going to take up a fair part of the rest of your life, therefore getting that part right will, I'm sure, be a huge part of your happiness. My challenge for you is to write ten things that a 'dream job' would entail for you and then put them in order of importance, one through ten. Just as I was, you may be surprised by what it is you're really looking for, and how you may or may not already be heading in the right direction. A realistic look will help to ensure you start pointing where you want to be.

That smile tells me something about job satisfaction!

Lesson #48

Transient Shanghai

If you quizzed everyone in Shanghai on words they would use to describe the city, the word 'transient' would come up many times. It is often voiced in a negative way – complaints about the constant need to develop new friendships, and the ever-present feeling that one of your closest friends is going to disappear at virtually no notice. A whole social calendar could be filled with leaving dinners and parties, but I guess that is what comes of there being so many students, interns, and employees often working on short-term contracts here.

This matches how the city itself is: constantly expanding, developing, growing, and changing. Streets often radically change their appearance, with new buildings, shops and restaurants popping up seemingly daily. At the beginning I saw this as a big annoyance. I found it frustrating then, but now I have flipped it around and started seeing it from another viewpoint.

Now, I see myself as living in a city where there are always new people arriving and starting their China experience. It is so interesting to see yourself becoming the 'old hand', able to help with these newcomers and their lack of Chinese knowledge. If you go out to a bar or club to meet new people, the vibe rivals Fresher's Week at University, except that it isn't just a week long.

Additionally, because friendship spans are often shorter, the speed of getting to know people increases rapidly. Many of us travel with people we haven't known for very long, and close bonds appear so fast; you hang out with groups where you know hardly anybody at first, and spontaneity is the name of the game. In fact, a large part of how I have been able to see and do so many interesting things is because so many of the people around me are fresh and wanting to explore – and if one set of friends doesn't want to visit a certain place or country, many others will. What could potentially be seen as a huge negative of the city, leads to many situations that just wouldn't be possible somewhere with more stability.

Midi Music Festival, Suzhou, Eastern China

Action: I believe happiness is hugely related to how we choose to respond to events. The game of life can be a real range of ecstasy, disappointment, pain, joy, suspense, waiting, heartbreak, elation, confusion, disbelief, and much more. Everybody has dealt with all these emotions, yet some have an overall positive outlook regardless. I've highlighted just a few of the situations that I consciously decided to flip around; my challenge today is to write down 25 of your own. This may sound like a lot, but the more attention you pay to areas that you have the ability to perceive differently, the more you can change your accustomed thinking, and see potential and happiness in what were previously less positive scenarios.

TAIWANESE REALISATION OF THE DAY

The Taiwanese have to be some of the most selfless people I've ever met. Watching them play musical chairs on the metro, to ensure that anyone slightly older or less physically able than themselves is seated, was hilarious but also incredibly cute. I legitimately just watched one guy sit down, then give his seat up, be offered another, give that one up too, and then turn down the offer of one more!

Taiwan definitely beats Shanghai with their orderly queuing system!

CHINESE REALISATION OF THE DAY

Sometimes it's hard to keep a straight face. I'm taking a taxi back from the airport and the driver is visibly upset after I get in and the ride isn't very far away. It should only be around £5. He slams the accelerator and speeds off, driving as fast as possible, beeping his horn and constantly moaning and huffing. What I notice straightaway, but he doesn't until more than half the journey is done, is that he forgot to push the button to start the meter running. Thank you very much sir for a less than half price taxi and extra speedy service too. Welcome back to China!

CHINESE REALISATION OF THE DAY

I am so glad I live in Shanghai for a few reasons. Despite how cool Taiwan has been this week, there are a few reasons I love 'home' more. Reason #1: the fact stinky tofu has not become a thing here. Damn, that stuff is terrible!

CHINESE REALISATION OF THE DAY

Chinese people have very short-term memories when it comes to remembering their luggage. For the first time in a while of travelling around Asia, I've got checked luggage. Watching the conveyer belt go round, and the same people grabbing seemingly every bag of any colour and size, before realising it's not theirs and replacing it, is ridiculous!

CHINESE REALISATION OF THE DAY

I will never get my head around the money spending and saving habits of the Chinese. Our flight was delayed a few minutes today, not because of anything to do with the flight, plane, or supplies, but because a Chinese couple had bought ten bags of shopping from duty free. With the flight full and luggage bins full, hostesses were emptying all of the supplies (pillows, blankets etc.) to make space to stuff these bags in. I can't imagine how much had been spent on electronics, alcohol, cigarettes and perfume. Then, fast forward a few hours, and the same couple is at the back of a long queue for a crowded bus to take them back to Shanghai centre – a much slower option than taking a taxi. I imagine they spent hundreds, if not thousands, of pounds at the airport, and then saved £20 on transport home. Hmmm!

Lesson #49

Laughing until you cry

I love the little smile you get from the local restaurant owner when you compliment their food, even while they are still just about getting over the shock of having Westerners in their place. And the huge grin a child on the metro gives you as you engage them in a staring competition whilst pulling silly faces. Or the Chinese couple's laughter when they try responding to you in English and you react by telling them you 'speak no English' and that really you're Chinese.

I like that, in a small way, you can put a smile on the face of others with very little effort, and never really know how much, or how little, value that smile may have given the recipient. Maybe on more than one occasion I have been called a flirt but, realistically, in many of these cases this is just exactly how I am. That's not to say I haven't flirted though... maybe once or twice!

I've always been a bit of a people watcher, fascinated by those around me, and being in China is heaven on earth for those of us who are that way inclined. Every single moment of the day there is something going on, very different from what my mind is used to, which makes for some incredible stories and never a dull moment.

The last two days I have been in floods of tears multiple times – fortunately through laughter, rather than pain. I've had ridiculous conversations with massage therapists about the size of my bum compared to Chinese people's, plus a whole series of hilarious events on the metro, including a tentative guy not knowing where to stand, and a couple trying to squeeze into a seat gap way too small, which made me laugh so much that those around me started laughing hysterically as well. Laughter is infectious and, even though nobody really knew what we were laughing at (and, realistically, the original event wasn't even that funny) everyone left that metro ride in great spirits, even if only momentarily.

The brain recognises the muscles in your face that move when you smile and, in return, it releases chemicals called endorphins. These are released with smiles, laughs, and even fake smiles, and can lift your mood, act as a natural painkiller, help lower stress levels, spread contagiously, and make those around you beam too. They can also help the body to relax, the immune system to react quicker and more effectively, and increase the production of white blood cells. Plus they can make you look younger, improving your overall appearance as well as making you more approachable. I mean, who doesn't want to hang out with someone who's permanently wearing a huge smile?

Action: Make it a challenge to yourself to smile upon waking up. Think of three things that make you smile as you get out of bed, and start the day with a huge beam. During the day, try to laugh and smile like a small child, even if it means putting yourself slightly out of your comfort zone to achieve that. For the really daring of you, follow the example of a great YouTube video I watched, where one guy starts laughing at the bus stop for no reason. Within minutes, every single person at the bus stop is laughing along too. If you are feeling particularly adventurous, try this one in a lift. Whatever it is, try to give yourself some more smile-related crease lines on your face by the end of this week!

Lesson #50

Marginal gains

If you are one of those people who love the idea of New Year's resolutions, and the chance to start afresh, you would love the situation I have here. Within the eight weeks from 31st December, I have had no less than four new starts! In addition to my standard English New Year and birthday, I also can add in my 'Chinaversary' and Chinese New Year as more opportunities to set new goals if I feel so inclined.

As it happens though, I've never been a fan, and would much prefer to make the changes in my lifestyle as and when I want them! Myself and a friend have instead stuck with a process of 'weekly goals', where each week we change one small aspect of our behaviour, which, when combined with the following week's challenge, leads to a more substantial change somewhere down the line, but without feeling unattainable right now.

If my goal is to get in the best shape I've ever been in, that's not going to happen within a week, but something I did want to switch up a bit was the amount I was exercising and what I was eating. I've always been pretty health conscious and still look similar to when I first arrived here, despite enjoying so much good food, some mystery meat, and copious oil and rice at so many mealtimes. A few of my personal sticking points though include the fact I love a good dessert and cocktails, and have quite a large appetite! For me, eating and drinking is for enjoyment as well as for energy, so subsequently the idea of not being able to eat all of the foods I like, as a payoff for looking how I want to look, isn't particularly appealing.

> ***"A year from now, you'll wish you started today."***

What I've done instead is started monitoring a few marginal goals and adopted a variety of positive and well-developed lifestyle changes, which will help get me closer to my more distant goal. The feeling of success when you make a change in one small area also seems to lead to greater levels of commitment – not only to carry on the same challenge, but also to keep plugging towards the overall goal as new elements are added in.

Inspired by the work of Sir Dave Brailsford, coach to the British Olympic cycling squad, I have included: Making morning smoothies, including a bunch of vegetables; preparing my own lunches and snacks instead of the oily work food; doing more home cooking, and making a social event of it at the house; setting a water-drinking challenge with a friend, which means I'll drink the right amount each day or face a forfeit; noting how much I would normally spend on snacks, and putting this money into healthier, more expensive and imported treat foods; fitting in trips to the gym early before work, and adding in two exercises that I will do at home every day, which take a grand total of around five minutes.

View of The Bund, Shanghai, by night

None of these changes have been huge, life-altering moves requiring many hours, and I really don't feel that I have lost out in any way from them. However, when you combine all of these changes, I've found it very easy to keep it up, and the results show that lots of small steps do add up.

Consequences are another valuable tool for anyone, like me, who's competitive and hates to lose. The idea of having to report to someone and inform them of my progress, as well as the thought in the back of my mind that I would owe them a tidy of their apartment, foot massage, lunch, or some other forfeit, is often enough to keep me determined to carry on and not fail, even when my own motivation isn't enough.

The idea of chipping away at a task and making small steps forward will enable you to achieve even the most distant of challenges. You may also realise along the way that, with a little planning, these steps don't necessarily have to be boring and a chore. I've done similar things with my Chinese learning and, with the small goals I've set myself here, I know I'll progress in a great way – far more than by just having the one huge goal, way out there, of being able to communicate fluently.

Action: Pick a task in your life that you'd like to achieve. Now, write at least ten things you can do that, when combined, will move you closer to that point. Your challenge is to implement these areas in your life, one at a time. Just pick one first, maybe the most achievable, and stick with it for a few days until it feels like a small habit. Give yourself credit for the first little part and then move onto the next. The timeframe will be very individual but, by adding in these additional marginal gains frequently, before you know it, you will be firmly on track. As nice as it would be to lose 10% body fat, drop six dress sizes, triple your IQ, and get down to a scratch golfing handicap, all within a week, these goals are a bit far-fetched. Challenge yourself to tackle one small, manageable chunk of that big puzzle. If it's to lose 10% body fat, perhaps swap your morning fizzy drink for a glass of water, and do this for one week. By adopting a new behaviour each week, especially with peer accountability and consequences to spur you on, you'll soon discover that you're now a lot closer to that seemingly far-fetched goal.

Lesson #51

No better or worse... just now!

I've just moved house. After almost a year of living 30 minutes west of the city and taking the familiar post-work metro ride downtown most days of the week to socialise, I now live right in the thick of it. I've been envisaging this move since I arrived, for the ease of transport to so many activities, the proximity to friends, and to feel like I really live in Shanghai. The thought of never having to worry about the time of the last metro home, leaving places in a hurry, or taking expensive taxis from the middle of town is very welcome. As the year has progressed though, I've taken a more rounded perspective and learned to appreciate things about where I was. My time on the metro has provided many fun experiences and conversations, as well as Chinese study time, and I had easy access to work so was always able to pop home at lunch to pick up another layer, put my washing out, or anything else that needed doing.* My new house will make my second year different to my first. Not necessarily better, just different.

Recently, I've spent time with friends and their siblings who are so different in almost every single way, yet both loved in their uniqueness by everyone around them; I've compared places I've visited and attempted to decide which one would be most liveable for me; I've chatted to friends about the career paths they've taken so far, many of them a long way away from their predictions; and I've reflected on jobs that I myself have not taken, and wondered where I would have ended up if I had.

It is interesting to imagine what would happen if there were parallel universes, but really I've come to the conclusion that there is no such thing as better and worse, just different. Different ways and opportunities to gain new experiences; even when your path diverges far from your original plan, it is still hugely useful for developing and becoming the best version of you possible. Being able to look at different and new experiences as just that, instead of comparing them to a previously experienced situation is one sure fire way to stay more positive and realistic.

I spent time on the plane to China picturing things I was glad to be leaving behind. Restricted job opportunities and career progressions, and familiar cultures and language, were a few of the things that as much as I love home, I wanted to switch up. Simply accepting pros and cons of both places, as opposed to getting frustrated when something is not as it was back home, is one reason why, almost a year in, I still feel like I'm in the honeymoon period and haven't turned into a grumpy expat just yet!

Action: This week, every time you discover or think of a negative about a situation you find yourself in, try to counter it with two positives and note the results. Everything has a mix of ups and downs; having these counter points in written form will solidify your thoughts, reminding you that, despite some less than ideal times, there are many positives in the decision you've made, so try and soak up all of the goodness from where you find yourself currently.

(* Who am I kidding? I am an expat and therefore pay an āyí/cleaner, who puts my washing out and takes care of everything, making me worry whether I will be able to function without her!)

Lesson #52

When perfect isn't good enough

One of my tasks at the academy, within my coaching role, is running the junior programme. I never anticipated how much time and work this would entail, but it is a lot of fun and very rewarding. Writing lesson plans, parent manuals, books and practice schedules; sourcing equipment; training other instructors; liaising with parents; updating the programme we offer; as well as my own research and training to ensure I can offer the best possible service – all of this goes alongside my increasingly busy coaching hours. It's a challenge, but a challenge I love, and it's all worth it whenever I see the progress of young golfers, the team of instructors delivering the lesson plans, or when I hear feedback from juniors or their parents and am able to step back and admire the results.

Out of all those challenges, the biggest of all is the fact I am a huge perfectionist.

In a quest to offer the absolute best junior programme, I spend lots of time reading books, articles and notes; Skyping all of the best coaches I am fortunate to have as friends; chatting with those I work alongside and the juniors I coach; and then consulting people way outside the world of golf for their unique opinions. All of this can quite easily leave me with lots of ideas, but also feeling overwhelmed and unable to take action. A few months ago, that was definitely the case.

Imagine how badly Apple would be failing if they hadn't created a phone until they'd developed all the features of the current iPhone. They would have wasted so many years of being able to gather feedback, develop, and letting their creativity decide just what a phone can become. Similarly with my plans, despite wanting them to be perfect, the best way I've found to achieve something is to get it written down and try it out in action. Then reflect; keep what you like, add in what you'd like more of and, before long, you'll be left with something far greater than if you keep expecting to put out a flawless first and final draft.

As obvious as I'm sure this message appears, the more I think of the great inventions of the world, and how many failures were involved, the more I realise these weren't failures, just stepping-stones. As I still see signs of my original lesson plans in the current versions, I anticipate that they will change greatly as I keep reflecting, and that's just fine!

Action: Think of a big project you have completed; perhaps a challenge at school, college, university or work, or even a personal goal. Write down how the initial few steps of this made you feel and what you experienced. This should help you appreciate just how far you moved forward in that area, and should also help next time it's tough to get started, when the perfectionist within you sees the goal as a lofty one with endless steps leading up to it.

On a side note, take a step back once in a while and give yourself a pat on the back for some of the things you're achieving; you're awesome.

CHINESE REALISATION OF THE DAY

A mutual scream is a good way to bond with your neighbour on the last day of staying in your place. I'd just popped outside my door, into the stairwell, to put out a bag of rubbish. Apparently, so did my neighbour. For such a short trip, neither of us bothered to turn the light on. As I turned the corner, out of the blackness I saw a face, and let's just say she wasn't expecting to see me either. The resulting mutual scream, embarrassed chuckle, and finally raucous laughter we shared were priceless. Too many confused emotions to process right now!

CHINESE REALISATION OF THE DAY

MANY Chinese couples really do not appear to like spending time with each other! On many occasions, I've watched scenes like this playing out; couples spend most of the time that they're 'out' with their other half scrolling through WeChat, only pausing to take a few selfies, snap food pictures and, in any spare moments, eat their food. If there is ANY other spare time not accounted for then maybe, just maybe, there will be some conversation. Not sure whether to laugh or just be shocked at what I see...

CHINESE REALISATION OF THE DAY

Apparently the Chinese are pretty fond of Photoshop and the touching up of photos. Yesterday I found a little shop where I could get pictures taken for a new visa for my upcoming travels. Fingers crossed that these photos will actually be recognised as me...The amount of Photoshop the old guy did to remove any lines, and make my skin clearer and a little paler, amongst other things, means it doesn't actually look much like me... I didn't stop him, only because I was laughing too much at the ridiculousness of it!

CHINESE REALISATION OF THE DAY

Chinese people when they are embarrassed are unbelievably cute. Today I am in a Chinese lesson and all is going well until I say something, my teacher goes quiet, looks at me with a slight awkward grin and then, after trying to suss me out, laughs hysterically for a good few minutes. Despite trying, she couldn't actually speak for that whole time, so I was left in the dark as to what I possibly could have said. Apparently the word 'shang' has quite a few meanings, and my attempt at telling her I was busy and had 13 hours of golf lessons over the weekend, actually came out that I was busy having an orgy with 13 of my students this weekend... As I realised what had happened, I decided to play along with the joke. I told her that was indeed true, and it was a very busy weekend. Her face was an absolute picture!

CHINESE REALISATION OF THE DAY

The final details often gets missed out here in China. I am in a brand new hotel and it has a plush walk in shower. Warm water, comfortable and everything is good. However, having a plug that drains water at the top of a slightly downward sloping floor leads to a constantly flooded room after use... hmmmmm!

ENGLISH REALISATION OF THE DAY

It's good to be home. In the first five minutes I saw more black people than during the whole of my first year in China. I am constantly surprised at the thought that everyone around me can understand English. It is raining. All is well!

Bonus Lesson #53

I'm 'home'

A couple of weeks ago I came 'home' to Shanghai after a ridiculously hectic ten days in England, where it was great to catch up with family, friends and fellow golf coaches, My diary was so packed I hardly had time to sleep, let alone think, but my abiding memory is of the same questions, put in many different ways: 'how is China?' and 'how long will you stay?'

On my return, I read through many of the stories and posts from my initial weeks in China and reflected on them with others, and I realised just how far I have come. For sure, I am not the same person who left England a little over a year ago.

I've returned even more determined to grasp every opportunity that comes up, only this time with the mind-set that China is not just an extended trip that may end any time soon; this really is home.

So the adventure continues: more magazine articles and my first live TV show, talking about golf in China and our academy. I am continuing to improve my language skills, dealing with customers and making sales, and even becoming more aware of which area of coaching I want to specialise in. The academy is moving in many new and exciting directions with new locations and much more in the pipeline. The junior academy I manage is growing and succeeding, and we are working with many of the top Chinese golfers. A few friends have stopped by in Shanghai recently, and there are more visitors planned in the next few months. I've also met some really great people, who have made life here even richer; I've set myself a few new personal challenges; and, to top it all off, summer is arriving!

When I look at all I've been able to achieve, it astounds me. I look at the endless opportunities in front of me and it is just incredible. But it all started with one decision.

Take a look at these words, which you may have seen before. They were written in the first story of this very same book. I can safely say that I took action and it has paid off; I would love you to do the same:

> *"If I do stay 'safe' within my comfort zone, turn back off the plane now, and live out the rest of my life in England, it would rid me of the short-term anxiety, but that is neither what I want to do, nor what is best for me right now.*
>
> *Picture one area or aspect of your life that is potentially scary right now. Try imagining what it could look like retrospectively, in a few years' time, if you stuck with it and allowed some of that initial discomfort to lead you in some new direction you've maybe never even thought of."*

Action: Enjoy the past, look forward to the future, but be happy in the present. Who knows what will happen next? I certainly didn't know that I would come to label China 'home', even though I knew I was moving there. Life changes, people change; enjoy now, it is the only time you will ever experience it. Whilst you're there, make now the best possible now that you can.

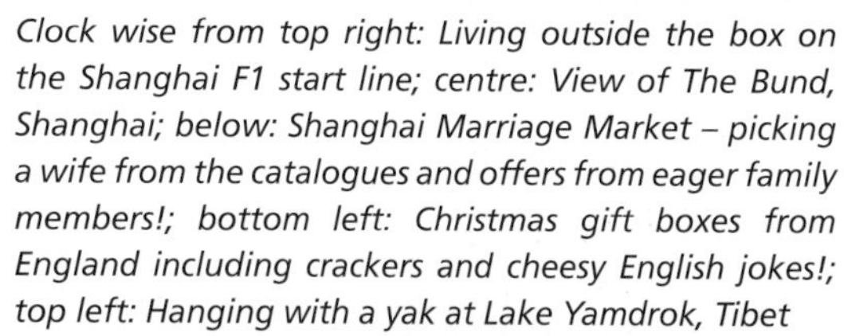

Clock wise from top right: Living outside the box on the Shanghai F1 start line; centre: View of The Bund, Shanghai; below: Shanghai Marriage Market – picking a wife from the catalogues and offers from eager family members!; bottom left: Christmas gift boxes from England including crackers and cheesy English jokes!; top left: Hanging with a yak at Lake Yamdrok, Tibet

Epilogue

As you've read this book, you've followed my experiences and my growth as I settle into life in this country. In my first year, since touching down in the Middle Kingdom, it is phenomenal for me to see how much I've transformed both personally and professionally, and also how well I've been able to adapt and thrive in a world so different to the UK.

As I write this, I have still only recently returned to China after a whirlwind trip back to the UK for catch-ups with family and friends, the wedding of one of my best friends, and lots of home comforts! For sure, I enjoyed seeing some of the huge differences about being back 'home' now that I've now become so accustomed to the way of life over here, but it has also been great to get back to the exhilaration, madness and unpredictability of China.

Ostrich riding, Vietnam

As 'normal' as living here can appear once you get used to it, I hope my future years leave me with just as many stories – perhaps enough to compile another book! I'm honoured you took part in this journey with me, in a small way, and hope that what you've read and actioned can also make a real difference in your life.

I truly believe we can find learning points in almost anything that happens in life. It doesn't require moving to the other side of the world, that's for sure. What I would say is that living and learning through your own and others' experiences will help you to grow, develop, evolve and become the best version of you possible. As my introduction alluded to, I hope that you (yes, **YOU**), the unique and perfectly created bundle of superbness can, in your ever-improving way, also leave the world a little bit better than when you found it.